Praise for *You Had*

"Jess Bugg is our canary in the coal mine. A true empath, she absorbs the environmental insults around us and implores us to share in her ecological grief. But all is not lost. Bugg's profound insights and actionable wisdom compel us to confront our ecological responsibilities head-on, reminding us that collective action holds the key to a sustainable future."—**Michael J. Ryan**, author of *A Taste for the Beautiful*

"*You Had to Be There* is a beautifully rendered personal experience of humanity's kinship with non-human animals and the planet. With captivating honesty, Jess interprets environmental crises with empathy for all those affected in a style that is both straightforward and poetic, philosophical yet down-to-Earth. This book has reinspired my own dedication to speak for those who cannot."
—**Bill Hatcher, author of** *The Red Planet*

"Adorno viewed the essay form as the embodiment of contradictions, and in this impressively substantial and thoughtful collection of linked essays Jess Bugg does exactly that, with reference to her/our confused/confusing response/non-response to the Anthropocene. Depressing/exhilarating."—**David Shields**, author of *The Very Last Interview*

"*You Had to Be There* felt like a conversation I've been yearning to have for the past 20 years. I haven't observed anyone explain veganism in all its facets with such depth and truth."—**Dr. Lauren Sanchez**, ND

"Engaging and beautifully written, *You Had to Be There* reveals Jess Bugg's talent for finding simplicity in the philosophical."—**Drew Nellins Smith**, author of *Arcade*

"The etymology of grief is to burden. The burden the Anthropocene puts on nature, our collective biology we grieve. Jess Bugg is an emergent personal voice to the viscerality of that grief; her essays an ethos of care as a way forward."—**Joel Fleschman**, LCSW

You Had to Be There

Thoughts on Ecological Grief in the Anthropocene

Jess Bugg

Lantern Publishing & Media • Woodstock and Brooklyn, NY

2024
Lantern Publishing & Media
PO Box 1350
Woodstock, NY 12498
www.lanternpm.org

Printed in the United States of America

Library of Congress Cataloging-in-Publication Data

Names: Bugg, Jess, author.
Title: You had to be there : ecological grief in the Anthropocene / Jess Bugg.
Description: Woodstock, NY : Lantern Publishing & Media, 2024. | Includes
    bibliographical references.
Identifiers: LCCN 2023054538 (print) | LCCN 2023054539 (ebook) | ISBN
    9781590567340 (paperback) | ISBN 9781590567357 (epub)
Subjects: LCSH: Environmental degradation--Psychological aspects. | Global
    environmental change—Psychological aspects. | Grief. | Loss (Psychology) |
    Nature—Effect of human beings on. | BISAC: NATURE / Environmental
    Conservation & Protection | PHILOSOPHY / Ethics & Moral Philosophy
Classification: LCC GE140 .B85 2024 (print) | LCC GE140 (ebook) | DDC
    304.2/8019—dc23/eng/20240709
LC record available at https://lccn.loc.gov/2023054538
LC ebook record available at https://lccn.loc.gov/2023054539

For Bones and Captain

There may be more beautiful times, but this one is ours.
—Jean-Paul Sartre

Contents

Introduction:
Living Grief

When I initially started working on this book, I wanted to travel to beautiful places and spend time in a very specific kind of nature—even though one of the points I was trying to make was that there are problems with this kind of thinking, and that nature is not a "separate place" one can go. Yet I still somehow felt compelled to be surrounded by landscapes that I don't regularly encounter. I thought I needed to isolate myself from humans and human noise in order to fully understand my own grief around the climate crisis.

However, traveling to these "pristine" places for the purpose of understanding the climate crisis only reinforced for me the problematic idea of separation—that this crisis is somehow not a part of my everyday life, that it takes place *away* from home. In reality, I know I am surrounded by non-human animals, people, plants, and natural places that, just like me, are suffering the effects of climate change. And although I am writing about the tendency many people have to separate themselves from nature, I am not immune to the pitfalls of this way of thinking.

Because I am focusing on my own experience with ecological grief, I will try my best not to write as a disembodied voice. I am certainly not the first to note, the terms *we*, *our*, and *us* are polarizing and inappropriate in most cases, however, I feel that in reference to the Anthropocene they are often the only words that make sense. *We* is used in reference to our current geological age in which *we* (humans) are the dominant influence on the environment. *We* is a distinction separating *Homo sapiens* from plants and non-human animals, in terms of our dominion over climate. *We* isn't meant to place blame on those causing the least amount of harm, who often actually suffer the most. It is well documented that the most privileged are leading the charge in this devastation.

The Anthropocene is a product of human-created cultures—*our* habits, *our* behaviors, and *our* relationship to non-human animals and the land around *us*. The decline of *our* home planet is, fundamentally, a shared experience. Because this book also explores the importance of respect toward non-human animals and is a reflection of my own beliefs regarding the treatment of non-human animals, I refrain from referring to any creature as "it." The only time I may use "it" in reference to a non-human animal is when quoting an author who used the term.

While I reference "ecological grief" throughout, it is somewhat of a catchall for grief related to life in the Anthropocene. Separation from nature, the rupture of bonds between humans and animals, displacement, biodiversity loss, anticipation of loss, excessive consumption, and a reliance on technology are all forms of grief that I categorize under the umbrella of "ecological grief." Using vocabulary associated with more familiar forms of grief to describe ecological grief is an attempt to begin a conversation about something I've found difficult to define.

When I began writing down my thoughts on ecological grief, I wasn't aware that it had any definition or had been discussed in any meaningful way. I was simply grasping for words to express the intangible feeling of loss and helplessness that had recently overcome me. Ecological grief is difficult to define as it is constantly evolving as we experience new forms of trauma. Climate disasters and environmental losses have increased alongside the growing immediacy of media and the ability to witness this worldwide tragedy in real time. For as long as I can remember, I've felt what I consider to be a manageable level of sadness over climate change; however, in recent years it has evolved into something new. The definition that most resonates with me is, "The grief felt in relation to experienced or anticipated ecological losses, including the loss of species, ecosystems and meaningful landscapes due to acute or chronic environmental change."[1]

I've experienced the grief of change, the loss of loved ones, losing my footing and sense of self. I often feel heartache over the losses I know are still to come. I've felt the physical pain of grief, the kind that permeates the core and settles in the bones. And while it may lie dormant at times, it is easily stirred into reanimation from the subtlest change in light or a familiar smell. But grieving the loss of our planet and way of life can sometimes be more difficult to accept; indeed, the magnitude of it is simply more than I can comprehend. It seems that in part, this grief is related to all the unknowns and that I don't know what it is I am actually grieving yet. It's a living grief that has no real form but concerns so much of life on earth.

With ecological grief there isn't a sense of definitive loss; rather, it's a confusing gray area that mostly lies in the anticipation of extreme loss and future hardships. It is the initial diagnosis that catches in the breath with the understanding that the future is not going to be what we thought. The confidence of yesterday is shattered and replaced with dread for tomorrow.

I can't remember a time when I wasn't aware of climate change, a problem I used to understand as "global warming" during my childhood in the 1990s. Now that we are living in a time when the climate crisis is front and center, the words of ecologist Aldo Leopold have achieved devastating relevance: "One of the penalties of an ecological education," he said, "is that one lives alone in a world of wounds."[2]

I often think of these words in relation to the climate crisis, for the vast majority of people have at least *some* understanding of climate change and are consciously or unconsciously receiving an ecological education. They are facing previously unseen levels of devastation on a regular basis, whether it's firsthand or indirectly through news sources, shipping delays, and empty store shelves.

I've experienced seasonal shifts—more heat waves, longer droughts, and harsher storms. I've experienced the secondhand loss of creatures and places I have never seen in person. Every time I travel somewhere new, it is inevitably the first conversation I have with a local. I hear about the increase in flooding from a bus driver or how certain produce isn't available that season due to drought. I stay inside more between the months of June and September or if I can, I will visit family located further from the equator. I have a box where I keep flashlights, freeze-dried foods, and other emergency items. These are not stored for some possible future threat but used regularly for annual disasters. In February of 2021, during the extreme winter storm in Texas, the grocery store shelves were emptied almost immediately. My partner, Evan, saw a single jar of salsa on the shelf of a local market, but decided to leave it for whoever had the tortilla chips.

Every choice I make in terms of food and household items reflects our current age, and every ingredient or material that enters our home is thoroughly vetted. But during the hours of a typical day, my personal life isn't interrupted by climate change. Not yet. I can't tell whether or not it's always in the back of my mind, ingrained in my body, creating a kind of permanent malaise. I think of myself as sharing a consciousness with all living beings and the earth itself, and so, I must ask myself, how could I not grieve from the sheer suffering of it all?

When looking further into the zeitgeist of the Anthropocene, it seems that both the media coverage of the topic and the medium with which we absorb it play a significant role not only in the perception of climate change, but also how we behave in relation to it. This collection is an exploration of my own experience with ecological grief in an effort to better understand these complex feelings and to perhaps embrace this new reality of life in the Anthropocene. By moving away from established narratives surrounding climate change I hope we, as a society, will be better equipped to reject what has proven thus far to be an ineffective response to our shared crisis, and find a new way of interacting with this abundant natural world, which, while grieving or not, we are still very much a part of.

Forest for the Trees

Blue

Late one winter afternoon I walked through the Metropolitan Museum of Art. In the long hall with all the white marble statues and green wooden folding chairs, I marveled more at the illumination of the statues than the statues themselves. Watching the light fade from the sky at twilight, it turned a rich cobalt that almost appeared phosphorescent—reminiscent of Pantone 293, I thought, although this hardly does it justice. This type of early evening blue appears the most vibrant when contrasted with a warm terrestrial glow like that of fireflies (or spotlights in a museum).

My eyes shifted from the brilliant sky through the glass ceiling to the lights reflecting off the marble, and I dreamed of someplace warm, far away from New York City. This had become something of a routine for me—the room, the colors, the hum of activity. It activated my imagination in a way that other, more intentional works of art did not.

I recalled variations of this color blue that I had encountered throughout my life: hanging low over the bonfires on the beaches of Santa Cruz; enveloping me as I jumped into the neighborhood pool one last time before closing; the last sunset I watched after three months spent in New Zealand. I stood on the edge of the ocean with new friends, talking until we faded into silhouettes. At numerous times in my life this color has come to represent different things. For much of my childhood, for instance, the color represented endings—the time when the streetlights turned on, signifying the end of play. Further into my teenage years and early twenties, it brought about a sense of excitement and endless possibilities, as the night was just beginning.

On this particular evening at the Met, however, it represented change itself. I watched the sky darken as a quiet panic coalesced at the crown of my head, dripping down my spine like a phantom egg yolk. I became struck with the awareness of time, a discomforting moment of consciousness usually drowned out by the nearest distraction. However, this time it crept up on me, and I was unable to escape.

Regardless of how much I willed this moment to remain, the evening rapidly gave way to night. I drew no solace from telling myself that the same color would return the following evening, because this particular shade of blue, on this particular evening, represented something more. I knew it would never return, just as I knew that the moment was lost forever. I could almost feel it slip from my fingertips like silt, or a shadow I had never really held to begin with. It was as if I stood on the end of a pier, watching a very large ship tip over. If only, by some optical illusion, I could just reach my hand out and put it right side up again; I was overcome by an irrational focus on fixing the unfixable, all the while knowing that the wake would soon reach me too.

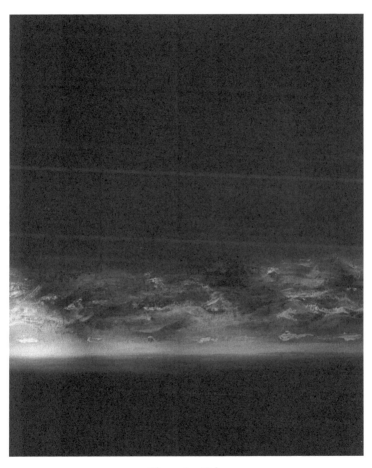

Change is a Color

Invisible Violence

I was homeschooled during my childhood, or, more accurately, unschooled. This isn't so uncommon today, but it was highly unusual in the 1990s—at least where I lived. I never reached the end of a grocery store checkout line without questions regarding my health, and the reason I wasn't in school. Even with my mother present there were many suspicious inquiries; I imagine they were meant as mini welfare checks. I was likely dirty—not from negligence, but from being outside, catching tadpoles and building forts. My afternoons were spent looking for the flowers with the brightest petals to dry in my press, or collecting berries to decorate pine cones with, turning them into miniature Christmas trees. I was relentless in my efforts to build a raft out of sticks that could hold my weight in the creek, even if it always immediately fell apart. I looked for the highest trees to climb, and often became stuck at the top. After a while, I would give up any hope of retrieval and would manage to find my way down again.

When friends were out of school in the summer, we would ride bikes after swim practice, stopping wherever there might be a good distraction. We rolled down hills until we were dizzy or biked to the small nearby lake to sit in other people's boats. I am not necessarily nostalgic over this time, but I know how lucky I am to have experienced this kind of childhood. I also wince thinking about all the creatures we unwittingly disturbed or harmed simply out of curiosity. All of those tadpoles that jumped out of my bucket and died on the garage floor overnight, or the doomed goose egg stolen from the nest because I believed it would hatch under my care, granting me a new best friend. Even as a small child, I held more power than these creatures who fell victim to my interest. While some lessons are best learned from books, rather than through firsthand experience, and this is especially true for lessons involving beings unable to speak for themselves, I am also aware that this sort of freewheeling, hands-on upbringing taught me to be more observant and empathetic; it taught me to love and respect this planet and the creatures we share it with. I knew all of the plants, insects, and animals that resided in my area. Completely enamored with the presence of nature around me, I felt connected in a way that I never questioned. As I grew older, those experiences became fewer and further between; but the foundation had been laid.

Given the fact that I was homeschooled, it is somewhat ironic that the school bus stop was directly in front of my house. In the afternoons I climbed the tree in my front yard, awaiting the arrival of the bus, eager to play with other kids and hear about the day's events and dramas that couldn't have been further from my own. In typical childhood fashion, I was often called names, and rumors abounded as to why I wasn't attending school. The children quizzed me on things they were learning about, knowing that I wouldn't have the answer. I mostly recall rhymes about Columbus discovering America and other troubling inaccuracies popular in American schools at the time. It didn't help that the only other homeschooled kids in the neighborhood were very religious, and never seemed to leave their front yard or play with anyone aside from their own siblings. There were five of them and they were pale, all with the same haircut. All of their names started with the letter K, which was unfortunate as my siblings and I have names starting with the letter J (pre-Kardashian fame, this was not a good look).

I was certainly not the most normal looking child, either. I cut my own hair and picked out my own clothing. If I found an outfit I liked, I wore it every day until I outgrew it, or my sister secretly discarded it from embarrassment. For years I wore a floor length denim dress with a white ruffled petticoat underneath, and a denim bucket hat that I pretended was a bonnet. Imagine seeing that up in a tree, reading a book at ten o'clock in the morning. I'm sure the neighborhood parents worried I would try to recruit their kids into some weird cult—and who could blame them? Luckily, I was good at sports, without which I am sure my social interactions would have proven far more difficult.

For holidays I would dress up in homemade costumes and beg my mom to take me on errands with her so the general public could see me in my elaborate outfits. The night before Valentine's Day I slept in curlers for my cherub costume, and for Christmas I dressed up as an elf. For hours I stood in the cold on our front porch, motionless except for the occasional, jerky wave. I held a basket of potpourri covered in string lights, hoping it would make me appear more animatronic. When a neighborhood friend later asked about our strange decorations, I beamed with pride.

Afternoons spent alone in the woods allowed my imagination to flourish, and I fully embraced whatever phase I was in without the mirror of my peers—at least until the bus arrived. I read a great deal of historical fiction, usually about the witch trials or pioneers; the American Girl series was also a favorite. For my birthday, I begged for hot pink rollerblades or a bike with shimmering tassels, but I was also well aware that these desires didn't resemble those of the characters that populated my books, and this troubled me. I wished so badly not to covet all that neon plastic, but I simply couldn't help it—it was just too tempting. If they were lucky, the heroines of my books would receive an orange or a peppermint stick, maybe some fabric to sew a dress with, and they'd be floored. I longed to be satisfied by such small pleasures.

Aside from some general aspects of childhood, the one thing I did share with these characters was the outdoors. It made me feel connected to the stories I was reading, and being in the woods granted me the freedom to imagine myself in another time or place. Occasionally I would set an early alarm so I could venture outside in the blueish predawn light described in my books. I sat outside, imagining people all over the world and all the generations prior who saw this light as they began their day. The experience made me long for some animals to feed. I wanted to elegantly scatter grains from a bucket and have little animals encircle me, like the illustrations in my storybooks.

For all the freedom and adventure available to me, I also came to know that I was incredibly naïve. That understanding led to an infatuation with my peers who, to me, resembled the kids on sitcoms. Becoming one of them felt key to my survival in the modern world. Their parents cooked spaghetti and made them finish their milk before leaving the table. They had endless processed snacks in their pantry, as well as Barbies and binders full of Pokémon cards. These kids had bedtimes, which is also why I rarely made it through the night during a sleepover. I would lie awake in the dark and imagine the lively glow of my own home where everyone would be awake, and my older siblings would likely have friends over that I could spy on.

While I had no interest in early bedtimes or being forced to down a full glass of cow's milk, I was envious of the structure that these families provided. I wanted to have the opportunity to complain about homework and rules and to pass notes or gossip about what happened in the cafeteria that day. I liked the performance of it all, but I couldn't authentically lose myself in the role because the other children knew that wasn't my life. Just based on my wardrobe alone, it was obvious I had no idea how to fit in. Perhaps the driving force behind my unshakable determination to leave home school behind and attend fourth grade was a desire to fit in, or maybe it was just another costume to try on; either way, I knew I wanted to experience the traditional American childhood that I saw portrayed on television. My parents reluctantly gave in, but I didn't even make it through the entire school year.

As soon as I started school, I began to feel sick. I had rarely suffered colds before, but this could easily be explained away by my exposure to a classroom full of kids and new germs. The classroom was located in a portable trailer with poor air circulation, which made it quite stuffy. The illnesses started with my cheeks, chest, and arms becoming red and blotchy. Then I developed flu-like symptoms. I was tired and achy all the time.

After staying home sick for a few days I would begin to feel better, but upon returning to class, I quickly fell ill again. I asked to see the school nurse almost daily, but my teacher thought I was faking ill in order to get out of class. I found this completely outlandish. I had begged endlessly to go to school in the first place, so the concept of faking an illness in order to leave never would have occurred to me. The teacher singled me out as a troublemaker and began calling on me constantly; given my fatigued state, however, my responses rarely pleased her, which only solidified her belief that I was a problem. In quintessential '90s fashion, I was deemed "diseased" by my classmates. I began to feel like a pariah, and my plan to transform into what I believed to be the average American child was foiled. After several months and numerous visits to the doctor, it was discovered that I was having a severe reaction to formaldehyde and other chemicals present in the newly built portable, and my doctor told my parents that I had to leave the school immediately.

My diagnosis coincided with my father's departure for a work trip to Maui, which then became an elaborate, three-week family vacation. I felt better with each day and rarely left the water. After eight months of what felt like the flu, it was a transformative experience. I let my body go limp in the ocean so the undertow could pull me under and tangle me up. The rush of not knowing when I would resurface was exhilarating. In a way, I think it was a form of coping with the confusion I felt over my illness. The waves allowed me to experiment with losing control in small increments, followed by the instant relief of breath. The strength of the ocean was also easier for me to understand than the equally disorienting exposure to invisible chemicals.

In the years that followed, I became increasingly sensitive both to chemicals and environmental allergens. During an overnight field trip to a science museum with my Girl Scout troop, I became severely ill from having my sleeping bag on the carpeted floor. I had always been a swimmer, but the chlorine from the pool suddenly become too overwhelming for me to continue training. The carpet in my bedroom had to be ripped out, because I developed a full body rash whenever I walked on it without shoes. Cleaning products and scented detergents gave me migraines, and even today I still feel faint around new construction and most scented materials.

Reminiscing about her own childhood experience with chemicals in the 1960s, my mom told me about the DDT mosquito trucks. She and kids all over the country would race to meet the trucks as they sprayed a thick fog of insecticide, enveloping them as they ran behind it. She said it was like the ice cream truck—

kids would come rushing out of their houses when they heard it approach. Even though DDT was banned in the 1970s, I imagine I inherited it, along with an increased sensitivity to chemicals from my parents, as DDT can be passed from one generation to the next. I began to visualize all the new chemicals attaching to my inherited ones, teaming up in an effort to destroy me. It seemed that toxins were everywhere and in everything—even in my own body. I became aware of the laundry list of chemicals and food additives legal in the United States but banned in many other countries. Even familiar snack food brands that are found worldwide contain harmful additives when sold in the U.S. but are reformulated without these chemicals when sold in other countries. For years I thought I was allergic to wheat because I became so ill whenever I ate foods containing it—but while traveling abroad, I was accidentally exposed and had no reaction. I was thrilled and continued to eat bread and pasta throughout the trip, assuming I had outgrown my allergy, but when I returned home it was just like before. Much later, I learned I was having a reaction to potassium bromate, an additive in flour that is widely used in the U.S. but banned in several countries including the European Union because it has been linked to cancer and is known to irritate the lungs and cause digestive issues.

Beginning with this brief stint as a fourth-grader, my life has been a series of intense illnesses followed by months, and sometimes years, of almost unblemished health. I never quite know when a malady will strike again, but routine colds don't always result in routine outcomes. Sometimes it seems as if the slightest wrong movement could once again awaken the alarm inside my body, telling it to overreact for the next several months.

At nineteen, I moved to New York City, but by twenty-three I was living with my parents again because I had become too sick to support myself. I had begun to sleep for fourteen hours a night, even sleeping through my alarms and missing shifts at work. Years later, after several false starts and a momentary reprieve from illness, I moved out on my own again and began dating Evan, now my husband. About a month into our relationship, we decided to plan a New Year's trip together. We discussed possible locations at length. Given our limited time and resources, we decided on a two-night stay at a hostel in West Texas. The hostel had several shared rooms as well as camping options. It also had an eccentric room for two that was located in a building a short distance from the main house, which we booked for our short holiday. The small room had a mattress on the floor and was covered in unusual antiques.

We arrived on New Year's Eve in the early evening to find that everyone was out celebrating at the local fire station, and so we had the place to ourselves. It was freezing that night, and we shivered as we cooked our dinner in the open-air kitchen. We both fell asleep shortly after midnight, but a couple of hours later I awoke with intense nausea. I was too queasy to walk from our room to the shared outdoor bathroom, and soon vomited outside the door of our room. I didn't want to wake Evan up, mostly because I was embarrassed. Everything was still new and romantic, and the last thing I wanted was for him to see me vomiting. He also had no knowledge of my medical history at this point, and I wasn't ready to divulge it. Eventually I made my way to the outdoor bathroom. My entire body would spasm as I vomited every fifteen minutes, passing out between each spasm. It was truly like clockwork.

I'm not sure how long this went on before Evan found me, but he began speaking to me through the door. I don't remember replying to him, but within minutes he was carrying me to the car and drove me to the nearest hospital. It took a while for them to see me, and I continued vomiting as we waited. Once I saw a doctor, the medical staff were able to stop the spasms by giving me a muscle relaxer through an IV. It was clear they assumed we had been partying and I was reacting to drugs—how every hospital visit would go from this point on. Evan ended up seeing me vomit many times that night, and he was also a witness to endless questions about my bowel movements and menstrual cycle, despite my best efforts to be discrete. The doctors carried out all kinds of tests on me that supplied no answers, but left me with a massive bill that took years to pay off, and ruined my credit.

These episodes continued to happen, and visits to the hospital assumed a familiar pattern. I would arrive and immediately have to explain that I didn't have the stomach flu or food poisoning and had not taken any drugs but just needed the vomiting to stop. I would then be sent on my way with prescriptions I never filled for various ailments I didn't have and receive bills in the mail for tests I never consented to. While these episodes seemed to occur at random, they always started out the same way: in the middle of the night when I was in a deep sleep. If I made it through the night, I knew I would be fine, which offered some relief.

Two years later Evan and I took a trip to Italy together. Whenever I experienced a stretch of good health, I eagerly planned trips and experiences because I never knew how long it would last and I didn't want to miss my window. I felt great during the entire trip, but on the way home I had an episode on the plane. I had unknowingly drifted off to sleep. While brief, I suppose it was a long enough nap to incite an episode. When I awoke with that familiar feeling of nausea I panicked. Fortunately, it was a short flight, as we had planned a long layover in Denmark so we could explore Copenhagen.

On arrival, we were put on an airport shuttle and rushed to a taxi so I could be taken to a hospital. I was brought into a room with big windows facing a courtyard and put on an IV. When I began to explain to the doctor that I wasn't on drugs and didn't have the stomach flu, she listened. She believed me when I told her it happened regularly but that I didn't know why. She didn't smirk, roll her eyes, or give me a prescription for something completely unrelated. She asked me questions about potential triggers, and as I spoke about the similarities surrounding my episodes, a clear pattern began to emerge and she explained what she believed was happening to me. Later I would discover that it was called cyclical vomiting syndrome.

The doctor gave me some muscle relaxers and told me to take them before I got on my next flight; there were enough to last a few weeks, and she told me to look for a specialist when I got back home. Evan had a chair by the window, and they brought him a sandwich and some juice; the staff told me to sleep until it was time for us to head back to the airport. We couldn't believe how peaceful it all felt, and how attentive the entire staff was. But when they left the room, we began to panic about payment—we didn't even know if we had enough money to get back to the airport. Evan went to speak with the front desk to explain our financial situation and beg for a reprieve. He came back in the room and whispered, "It's free." In our distressed state we had forgotten where we were and that universal healthcare existed. We breathed a sigh of relief, and I had the best nap of my life.

The episodes soon became hard to predict. They would generally happen either every two weeks, once a month, or sometimes up to six months apart. The interludes were not without symptoms, however; I suffered from nausea that ranged from mild to severe, and experienced migraines often. This made it difficult to keep a job, and I couldn't afford consistent health insurance during these years; even when I did have it, it didn't cover much, which drove me further into debt. After my hospital experience in Denmark, I found a doctor in the U.S. who prescribed me muscle relaxers, but they were not always reliable. I eventually learned that I could stop the vomiting myself after a couple of hours if I soaked in a hot bath, and this helped to cut costs. I also learned my specific triggers— cold temperatures while being overtired during menstruation is one—and, for the most part, I have been able to avoid episodes in recent years.

* * *

Writing about illness is difficult because my brain desperately wants me to forget. Occasionally someone unfamiliar with my past will ask me a question pertaining to childhood or my twenties that requires an explanation of my health or lack thereof and I struggle to put into words what was actually happening.

My instinct is to downplay how bad it was, because when I am not actively going through it, it's easier to pretend it doesn't exist. But I know that at certain points I believed my life was ending, and I know I lived in fear. I also know that I am still recovering in numerous ways: physically, mentally, spiritually, and, most annoying, financially. Our brains protect us from obsessing about death and what surrounds it as a survival tactic; if they didn't, we wouldn't get anything done. It's hard for me not to equate this to climate change because it, too, is a form of illness and death that I imagine our brains are trying to protect us from.

The underlying causes of cyclical vomiting syndrome are unknown, although there are possible links with hormone imbalances and nervous system issues, both of which are heavily impacted by chemical exposure. According to the EPA, the nervous system is especially affected by chemical exposure in early life.[3] Maybe it was the portable trailer in fourth grade, that neon plastic I loved so much, the DDT from my parents, the potassium bromate, or the thousands of other chemicals we are consistently exposed to. Maybe it was growing up in a society that doesn't know how to slow down and lives in conflict with the natural world. Or maybe it's completely random. My feelings about why all of this occurred are certainly anecdotal, but when there are no answers it's hard not to speculate.

I became aware of a shift in how I was perceived by others. When I developed food allergies, I was deemed a "picky eater." I was viewed as an overly sensitive, weak person. It frustrated me that it didn't seem to matter to those categorizing me in this way that none of this was in my control, and nor was it how I saw myself, but eventually I allowed this narrative to take hold. When you are viewed as frail, you aren't expected to be much else, and this in itself can be liberating. I experienced depression and anxiety about my illness, and constantly worried about triggering an episode, especially at inconvenient times. But, at the same time, when I was actually having the episodes, I almost experienced a sense of relief or calm. The attacks were horrifically painful, but it didn't matter. As I began to pass out, I felt content. The vomiting brought back sensations of being in the undertow as a child, and the passing out the relief of breath. I began to wonder if I was bringing this on myself. I was overcome with shame and guilt and sought out a therapist who specialized in chronic illness. I admitted this to him and he explained that, during an episode, there is no longer anxiety over the anticipation of having one because it is simply happening. The whole body is consumed by it. The anxiety of vomiting and passing out in front of strangers, the depression from feeling alone, the embarrassment of not being able to keep a job, worries about money and my future—all of these disappeared during an attack. I no longer thought about anything other than the moment I was in, and regardless of what I was experiencing, it brought peace.

I've often thought about the kids in that school who didn't react to the chemicals in the trailer. How many years did they spend in those buildings, unknowingly breathing in formaldehyde and other toxins? What if it was affecting them, just in less obvious ways? If they developed illnesses later in life, would anyone connect it back to that exposure in childhood? Is there even a connection to be made? What about those who live in mobile homes and do become ill but can't move or get help?

* * *

In her article "Alterlife and Decolonial Chemical Relations," Michelle Murphy at the University of Toronto confirms that this is a problem affecting everyone, not just a select few:

> Analyzing urine, blood, and breastmilk, twenty-first-century global biomonitoring studies have concluded that all people alive today contain PCBs [polychlorinated biphenyls] within them . . . industrially produced chemicals have become a part of human living-being.[4]

Murphy writes about the urban surfaces that collect PCBs, and the rainfall that washes them into bodies of water before they eventually find their way into our own. "The water is not still; it is indifferent to borders, cycling through the atmosphere, splashing off office towers, and returning to nourish humans, animals, and plants." On top of the toxins that have permanently infiltrated our bodies, how many new ones, we might ask, are waiting in the wings? How many do we choose to ignore?

When Evan and I discussed the possibility of having children, we played out all the usual worst-case scenarios that potential new parents contemplate. We questioned whether it was selfish given global overpopulation, what we imagine the future will look like, and their contribution to climate change. After years of circular discussions, philosophical debates, and reading a popular Ezra Klein *New York Times* opinion piece titled "Your Kids Are Not Doomed" about a dozen times, we decided to explore the topic more seriously.[5]

I discussed the possibility of having children and my fears regarding the physical aspects with my doctor. She told me to avoid all the usual dangers and known toxins, but also to make sure I didn't have a vinyl shower curtain, not to handle paper receipts, and to check the ingredients of every product in my house at least a few months before trying. All of these things, she warned, could contribute to infertility. If there is an awareness that these chemicals are causing infertility, shouldn't that tell us our bodies are not impenetrable—that we are directly absorbing our environment? And why on earth are we still producing these materials?

Given my own experience with chemical exposure and how it changed my health, I thought I was prepared and had considered every possibility, but there is simply too much to consider. My house was built in the 1970s; what about the lead-based paint and asbestos that was legal then and has since been outlawed? What about the vinyl flooring I can't afford to replace? What about trash bags, the cleaning products my gym uses, the scented soap from a public restroom, the glues that are in my running shoes? What about gardening—isn't soil full of contaminants? What about the dyes in my clothes? What about carbon dioxide when I am sitting in traffic, or the flame-retardant chemical in my sofa, our car seats, and our mattress? We had worried so much about future, exterior threats, and planned out worst-case scenarios, it's dizzying to contemplate all the ways in which we could be exposing a new and fragile life to the invisible violence of simply existing in our current age.

When the topic of climate change arises, it is typically viewed as a whole and what the outcome of it will be. But when dissected, it's billions of microscopic things breaking down. How do we categorize what is an effect of climate change—and what isn't? If all of the chemicals being pumped out by corporations and the consumption of fossil fuels is polluting our air, water, and soil, and in turn affecting both the climate and ourselves, then couldn't the unknown, underlying cause of my cyclical vomiting syndrome simply fall under climate change? Pollution kills several million people each year; if these deaths are directly related to climate change, which I believe they are, it doesn't seem like a stretch to consider that these toxins are causing even more harm than we realize.

In "Your Kids Are Not Doomed," Klein speaks about how bad things have been in the past and says that having children was always "an act of hope." He writes about pollution and how that too has lessened. He suggests that while climate change will certainly be bad, it is unlikely that life will ever be as bad as it was in the past:

> No mainstream climate models suggest a return to a world as bad as the one we had in 1950, to say nothing of 1150. Was the world so bad, for virtually the entirety of human history, that our ancestors shouldn't have made our lives possible? If not, then nothing in our near future looks so horrible that it turns reproduction into an immoral act.

He mentions that in his years of reporting on climate change he's noticed "the people who have devoted their lives to combating climate change keep having children." While I know this is meant to be reassuring, I am skeptical that even these climate devotees are immune to the pitfalls of human behavior. I've observed that people often do not behave in a way that matches their beliefs. Klein doesn't discount the horrors that climate change will surely bring. But if climate change in popular culture was shown as more than major disasters and extreme weather conditions—yes, we are often shown smokestacks, but if the reality of illness caused from these toxins was front and center—I believe it would open up a more nuanced conversation. Because while some of these toxins will certainly lessen in the coming decades, that doesn't change the fact that we are, in many cases, just beginning to understand the harm these pollutants have caused and will certainly be living with the fallout for years to come.

During the COVID-19 pandemic, I was afraid of getting sick; I was worried for my loved ones and society's most vulnerable. I worried about food shortages and money. From a different perspective, however, the reality of what was happening, and the shift to a new normal, had almost no effect on me. In some ways it came as a relief, because the worst was here and I no longer had to worry about it. The entire world was experiencing something terrifying, and the focus was on the moment. The results of our behavior were finally materializing in a way that everyone could clearly see, and I waited for a widespread shift in perspective. We no longer had to just theorize about the effects of the Anthropocene, or ponder how we might be impacted by climate change in the future; it was here in the form of illness. But then it wasn't. And just like with my own health issues, I understand the instinct to forget. But in the case of worldwide disturbance, it would suit us to remember.

In his 2012 book *Spillover: Animal Infections and the Next Human Pandemic*, David Quammen notes that "Ecological disturbance causes diseases to emerge. Shake a tree, and things fall out."[6] With so many bodies traveling to so many places, with landscapes reshaped and habitats disappearing, we were incredibly lucky to have made it so long without a worldwide pandemic. It seems reasonable to assume there will be many more in the coming years, as there appears to be no sign of societies slowing down. We have yet to figure out how to protect our home and fellow species from ourselves.

When it comes to my own exposure to chemicals in childhood, I know how good I had it. I was able to receive a relatively quick diagnosis and I was taken out of school. I went to Maui at the height of my illness, a level of privilege certainly not experienced by most. I could stay home because my mom didn't have to work outside the house for us to get by. When contemplating parenthood, I'm aware that my hypothetical child would not have anywhere near those same luxuries. I recently had to make a series of doctors' appointments for early next year, because at the moment I don't have health insurance—it was suspended when I missed a payment and could not afford to pay double the following month. I still haven't recovered financially from years of illness in my twenties, and even now I require more rest than I would like and am unable to work the number of hours I need to live comfortably.

When considering whether to bring another being into this world, it's hard not to visualize all the ways in which the body experiences violence. Through the altering of our environment, this violence goes beyond any kind of protection; how can I protect a child from an invisible force that has permeated our bodies? How many pandemics does the body have to fight through before lifestyle changes stick? I can't help but wonder if the experience of chronic illness and cancer will become a forgone conclusion for every member of American society.

My early childhood feels like a dream, one that I wish was more commonplace or available. The ability to wander in nature, unscheduled. A luxury that should be a basic right; that time was crucial in fostering my appreciation for my surroundings and the rhythms of the natural world. Yet, our society only seems to be pushing us further out of sync, and I worry that intrinsic bond will only continue to fracture in the generations to come.

Invisible Wounds

Observation Hurts

Hope Ryden was an American naturalist, photographer, documentary producer, and wildlife activist. She authored over twenty books on animals before she passed away in 2017. Jane Goodall said of her book *Lily Pond: Four Years with a Family of Beavers*, "Not only is it a major contribution to our understanding of the natural history of beavers, but it points to the value of detailed observation of individually known animals over long periods of time."[7]

The beavers that Ryden observed resided in a park near Ryden's home in upstate New York, allowing her to visit daily; she was also granted permission to stay in the park overnight, the period when beavers are most active. During her nights in the park, she came to realize that humans presented a greater threat to her safety than non-human animals after witnessing poachers, illegal hunters, and reckless campers. She observed people shooting fireworks at the beaver family on the Fourth of July, people looking for beaver kits to sell, and the aftermath of a vandal's destruction of the beaver dam. When she informed police officers of the dam's destruction—which they confirmed as a wanton act of aggression—the police replied that they were understaffed and unable to help. Ryden also mentioned that the police were immediately called away from the destroyed dam because of reports of a woman being molested in another area of the park. This detail only reinforces the continuous barrage of violence toward vulnerable beings.

Ryden discusses the history of the beaver; their evolution; their cultural importance among some Native American tribes; their population decline through European migration, industrialization, and fur trapping; and their eventual resurgence through conservation efforts. This history of the beaver is illuminated through the narrative of one beaver family that she describes as "gnomes, who work magic and transform their surroundings during the dark of night." She also includes photographs she took during her research, as well as maps drawn of their dams and the dams of offspring who took up residence in nearby ponds.

During her time at the dam, she watched a female beaver, whom she calls Laurel, from birth until two years old, when she was hit by a passing car. Ryden deeply mourns the loss of Laurel, not only from an ecological standpoint, but also as a witness to her life. She spent two years observing Laurel's parents work extremely hard raising her, especially through the harsh winters. She views Laurel's death as a "tragic waste" and asks, "How much natural selection and energy and experience and example and resource had gone into shaping Laurel? What provisions had been carried to her infant self, what biomass had been consumed, what risks had been taken, what care had been administered?"

Laurel had beaten the odds and survived all of the evolutionary tests that future generations would have benefitted from, if given the opportunity to procreate; however, a passing car ended all of that. Ryden feels anger toward people sneaking into the park, those speeding on the roads, and even toward the park rangers who fail to control them.

"Responsibility for such unabated slaughter," she writes, "must reside with us, collectively and individually, no matter how we avert our eyes and deny the gory evidence of our carelessness." Ryden tries to sympathize with the driver and imagines how awful they might feel, in order to calm herself down. Later that day Ryden returns to the dam Laurel and her mate (whom she calls Skipper) were building. She watches as Skipper continues to build the dam alone, unaware that his mate is dead. The next day he abandons the dam and moves back to the family dam he grew up in.

Although Ryden simply recounts these events, her personal anguish and attention to every detail of these beavers' lives is what makes this story so compelling. It is heartbreaking to imagine this young beaver couple straight out of the watercolor pages of Beatrix Potter, building their new home and preparing to raise their young together, only for it all to be taken away. While these events did actually take place, my mind is certainly anthropomorphizing the beavers beyond what Ryden is describing. However, I would argue that (in most cases) this is a positive thing, and I appreciate Ryden for allowing the space to do so. Being told that we shouldn't anthropomorphize is the same to me as saying: these non-human animals are too different from human animals, and therefore any human characteristics found within the species should be ignored. Yet, the more I learn about non-human animals, the clearer I see my own species. I often find there are many more similarities than differences. I don't see any issue with anthropomorphizing the beavers in this case because it doesn't change the information; it only makes me relate to the beavers and feel more empathy toward beavers as a species, rather than simply absorbing the information as completely separate. It's hard not to think about this beaver family, and about all of the trials they faced in the four years that Ryden observed them, and not think about all the other countless, unnecessary tragedies that might have occurred after her time with them ended. When people disrupt the beavers and their dam, Ryden is the only one around to see it. She intervenes when possible, but at other times she is forced to remain hidden out of concern that individuals may turn their aggression toward her. The park was closed at night and monitored by rangers, yet these beavers could not escape human violence.

When the matriarch of the family becomes ill, Ryden alerts the park in the hopes of administering medicine. However, she is told they cannot intervene, that *nature must take its course*. One of the themes in Ryden's book is centered around the idea of intervention. She is told nothing can be done for the beaver, because her illness is natural. Yet, nothing is done about the beaver deaths she doesn't consider natural—such as Laurel being hit by a car. She questions when they would find it appropriate to intervene.

For example, before the pond freezes over, and the beavers are limited during the winter to their dam and the water just beneath it, they stockpile branches and various flora to eat over winter. Ryden notes that this process weeds out the weakest of the species, and lends itself to the betterment of the beavers overall. From this perspective, helping them would only teach them not to collect enough the next winter. But when she realizes the beaver family she has come to love is failing to stockpile enough food for winter, she agonizes over it. She believes the reason they weren't able to collect enough is because of the time spent mending their (human destroyed) dam. Once the pond freezes over, and the winter shows no signs of abating, she decides to cut a hole in the ice and leave bundles of branches by it for the beavers to retrieve, which they promptly do. She justifies this intervention by considering that other humans would have been the root cause of their starvation by interrupting their process earlier in the season. Their failure to stockpile enough food was not due to the weakness of their bloodline. Ryden also contemplates all the other ways in which humans are contributing to the death of wildlife in general, and wonders if helping a beaver family survive the winter is all that detrimental to the species when all she is doing is making up for some of the more unnatural dangers. When spring finally arrives, and the ice thaws, Ryden comes to realize that the beavers had large amounts of water lily rhizomes underneath their den, and that, in fact, they knew that they didn't need to stockpile as many branches for the winter because of this reserve. Ryden's gift of branches turned out to be a welcome but unnecessary mid-winter snack.

Ryden worried that her presence at the pond might cause the beavers to become desensitized to humans. After witnessing so many aggressive people in the park, this became an even larger concern. As a result, she decides to use the beaver's own tactics of slapping the water as a warning to warn them against herself. It's not until the matriarch of the family is dying that she breaks from this stance and comes close to her, feeding her a favorite food of aspen branches.

* * *

While traveling through Europe, the writer Elisabeth Tova Bailey became afflicted with a mysterious pathogen that rendered her almost completely paralyzed. She learned that her autonomic nervous system was damaged, and that the mitochondria in her cells no longer functioned. Beyond this, she was given no further answers about her illness. Her world was suddenly condensed to a single bed. At times, she was barely able to turn her head. She documents this experience in her 2010 book *The Sound of a Wild Snail Eating*, writing: "The search is exhaustive; the answers, elusive. Sometimes my mind went blank and listless; at other times it was flooded with storms of thought, unspeakable sadness, and intolerable loss."[8]

In an effort to cheer her up, a visiting friend dug up some flowers and placed them in a pot by her bedside. With them was a snail. At first Bailey was annoyed that her friend captured this snail; she had no use for a snail and did not have the capacity to take care of one. She also felt guilty that this snail was taken from their home only to be confined to this isolated space with her. She couldn't remember having ever noticed a snail on her countless hikes over the years, but now, restricted to her one position, she ended up watching the snail every day. Commenting on the situation that she and the snail have somehow found themselves in, she wrote that "The snail and I were both living in altered landscapes not of our choosing; I figured we shared a sense of loss and displacement."

Over time, Bailey developed a kinship with the snail, learning their preferences and trying her best to accommodate. She requested various foods for the snail, and eventually acquired a large tank with the flora from the snail's home. Given her current state, her sense of time and space had changed and friends' behavior became overwhelming. She noticed their discomfort with stillness and how much they moved and fidgeted. She also noticed their discomfort with her, noting that "They would worry about wearing me out, but I could also see that I was a reminder of all they feared: chance, uncertainty, loss, and the sharp edge of mortality." The snail became a more comforting companion.

The nights gave Bailey a sense of solace, as knowing healthy people were also returning to their own beds made her feel less alone. Yet her nights were often sleepless, and the snail's nocturnal habits filled in the gaps caused by her loneliness. Absorbed in the snail's every movement, time began to pass more quickly for her and felt less like a cruel punishment. She was able to step out of her own suffering by embracing the snail's pace, admiring their genetic makeup and finding similarities with her own species. During the course of her illness, the snail also had several offspring. She states, "I was certain that my snail was just as aware of the details of its world as I was of mine, and so I began to wonder about its intelligence." She learns that snails have memory, can learn new tastes and smells, can retain knowledge for months, and even adapt their behavior to fit their particular situation. Bailey learned about snail farming for food production, and that snails will often form an aggregate, working in unison to push the lids off their tightly packed boxes to escape confinement.

Over time, Bailey's condition became manageable, and her snail was released back to the place where they were first found along with their offspring—except for one, which she kept a little while longer as she readjusted to her new, more mobile life.

* * *

Caring for other mammals is typically the most natural jump for humans (aside from the mammals we eat who are not valued beyond their being a food source). Non-human mammals obviously share many of the same traits as us and are therefore easier to relate to than a snail. A snail is almost invisible; perhaps it's their size or because they are harder to differentiate from others in their species—or perhaps it's because much of a snail's ecological significance is simply being food for other animals. I am skeptical that the human preference for one creature over another is based on anything other than conditioning, lazy tradition, and absurdity. Unfortunately, our baseless preferences have the power to dictate how animals are treated. Even so, that doesn't change the importance of an individual being or species, ecologically or spiritually.

There are snails all over my garden. In the morning, I often find their pearlescent trails adorning my flower pots. Before reading Bailey's story, I rarely stopped to watch them for more than a few seconds at time. A snail is an unlikely companion for *Homo sapiens*, but Bailey, like Ryden, shows us the power of simple observation and how it can shift our perspective.

The snail's presence in her life during this difficult time kept her in the present moment; observing the snail's every movement, together with her new curiosity about the life of snails, freed her from the pain of her situation and the longing for her past life. She was able to accept her new reality by relating it to the life of a snail. The snail shifted her perspective on what a life could be and allowed her to focus on something beyond herself and care for a creature she previously thought nothing about. I'd argue that being moved to care for someone beyond oneself, especially another species so different from our own, is a noble first step in moving through our climate grief. It can be an incredibly grounding experience, one that leads to an understanding of our role as humans into a place of acceptance of the crisis we've created. It has the power to shift feelings of guilt and hopelessness into meaningful action.

Bailey's situation is of course different than that described by Ryden—the snail was plucked from their natural habitat against their will and given to her against hers. No intervention in the snail's life was necessary; in fact, it was she who needed the help from the snail. The snail helped Bailey tremendously during her time of suffering, and she wants others to recognize how incredible the species is by sharing the story of her relationship with the snail. She spends multiple chapters on the life of the snail, the distinct differences between snail species, and their importance in the world. A garden snail is not an exciting creature in our culture, or on the verge of extinction, but Bailey treats snails just the same.

Often our hurried lives don't allow for observation of our surroundings, and without observation intervention won't take place. Changing our pace to match that of another species suddenly opens up new worlds of understanding and inexhaustible opportunities to create meaning.

Everywhere and Nowhere

Small Interventions

A few years ago, I went on vacation to Kauai with my partner, Evan. Feral chickens abound on the island, an apparent consequence of two hurricanes (1982 and 1992) that destroyed the coops of domesticated chickens.[9] These chickens then bred with wild red jungle fowl, which were originally brought to the islands by the Polynesians. I had never really seen chickens up close before this trip—I had maybe seen them a few times in someone's backyard coop—and encountering them in grocery store parking lots, on hiking trails, and at the beach was a new experience. At an outdoor juice bar, a hen followed by four fuzzy chicks huddled under our table, waiting for scraps. The little chicks were adorable, and it was hard not to pick them up and cuddle them. I was previously aware of the plight of the chicken in regard to industrialized farming, and it had been many years since I viewed them as food, but I didn't particularly think of their individuality.

During our trip, we rented a house in Anahola for five days. One morning, we heard a loud shriek outside. We had become used to the sounds of roosters crowing at dawn, and squawks from hens throughout the day, but this one was particularly loud. We almost laughed at the strangeness of it before realizing something was wrong. Evan looked out of the window and saw a dog in the distance, furiously shaking a hen in its jaws like a stuffed toy. Before we could even reach the back door, the dog had apparently grown bored once the chicken had fallen still, and had wandered off.

When we approached the hen, she looked up at us and I was upset she was still alive. I felt guilty for wishing she was dead, but I knew she had to be suffering and was likely beyond recovery. I retrieved a clean dishcloth from the pantry and wrapped her body in it, and then placed her in a cardboard box to keep her safe, while Evan and I discussed what to do. The hen made no sound, but seemed quite alert; it was difficult for me to tell how injured she was. The dog was large and seemed to have had a firm grip on her, but no blood seeped through her thick feathers.

We called the owners of the house, hoping they would know where to take her, but instead they seemed amused by the situation and explained that this happens all the time; she was a feral chicken that belonged to nobody, and so it was fine to just leave her there. We called shelters and sanctuaries that were either unreachable or stated they did not take chickens. We found a veterinarian about an hour south from where we were staying who agreed to see a "pet" chicken, so we headed over with our new family member.

In the car, I held the box in my lap and softly brushed the top of her head. She seemed to almost purr as she gently closed her eyes. I told the woman behind the counter about the hen's injury, and she informed me that she would most likely need to be put down, and then explained the necessary pricing. We took our seat alongside leashed dogs and cats in carriers, and received many side glances over our little chicken in a box. When they called us back, I told Evan to stay in the waiting room. I figured that we didn't both need to go through this experience which, by now, I sensed was going to be upsetting. At least, that's what I told myself in the moment;

looking back, I wonder if it was more selfish. I knew someday I would have to face the death of my adored pets, which at the time was my greatest fear. I didn't know how to process death or the grief that would come with it and needed to experience some form of it alone. I needed to know I could get through it.

The veterinarian and two assistants told me to place the hen in the middle of the table, and we all stood around her as the doctor lifted her wing and nonchalantly dropped it against the table, causing a small thud. As he explained the extent of her injuries, I placed my hands around her wings, hoping it would make her feel more secure and to discourage any further poking and prodding. The veterinarian explained that the treatment required for her injuries would likely cause her further stress, and she would most certainly die without someone constantly tending to her; even then, it was unlikely that she would make it. I told him we were leaving in 48 hours and asked whether he knew somewhere we could take her or anyone willing to care for her after we left. He did not.

We agreed that euthanasia would be the most humane option. Privately, I struggled with this decision and wished I could take her home with us; it didn't seem fair that we were making this decision for her. I gently held her and petted her head as he administered the shot. I cried as I watched her slowly fade away. I felt self-conscious over my grief and apologized, stating I understood that she was "just a chicken." I was immediatcly angry at myself and regretted saying it—I had given into the perceived pressure to undermine her life when I did not actually believe she was "just" anything; rather, she was an important individual I had just watched die. My grief was completely justified.

The doctor asked where I was from, and when I told him Texas, I saw his eyes soften. The assistant patted my arm as she handed me tissues. She told me she understood my grief, and that she imagined in Texas chickens must be very important to people and, to me, are probably more like pets. I smiled and nodded in agreement, as I was eager for any excuse.

As the doctor walked me to the front, he asked about my plans for the rest of our vacation, and with a discreet shake of his head, he told the woman behind the desk not to charge me. I thanked them profusely and apologized again for crying. In the car, I wondered aloud to Evan about their perception of us, and we laughed through our tears. Maybe they imagined us sitting on the sunken porch of a farmhouse, drinking sweet tea with our cows and flocks of chickens, as if we were straight out of a Walker Evans photo. I wondered if we would become an anecdote—the bumpkins from Texas who brought in a feral chicken as their pet. Or maybe they softened because we were tourists who were treating our new surroundings and their home with respect.

Later we went on a hike, and cried off and on the rest of the day whenever we thought of her. I never imagined shedding a tear over a chicken, but I still occasionally do whenever I think about her sitting in the tall grass—alone, hurt, and vulnerable. I had never really thought about chickens as individuals before; they were just one large, exploited group to me—but, of course, that changed after this experience and made me more passionate about their overall well-being.

On our last day we sat on the neighborhood beach where we had spent much of our time during the five-day trip. We brought trash bags and cleaned for a few hours, taking swim breaks in between. An older couple nodded as they passed us, looking for a place to set out their towels. As the sun set, we walked back to the house with our bags full of bottle caps, plastic Starbucks cups, scraps of fishing net, and flip-flops. We passed the couple again and noticed they had compiled their own garbage collection to take back with them and we all waved to each other in an act of camaraderie.

It was around 6 p.m. the next day when we arrived back in Austin. We were exhausted after our long trip, and still felt a little fragile after the experience with the chicken. We were eager to be comforted by our own pets and to wrap our arms around them. They were staying with Evan's parents, and we headed straight over to pick them up before driving home for dinner. A few blocks from their house, we came across a little chihuahua running down the middle of the street. We looked at each other and sighed as we slowly pulled the car over. We laughed so as not to cry over our exhaustion and the weight of our obligation to help.

Evan shouted, "Fuck people!" through gritted teeth as we got out of the car to call the dog over. The chihuahua was not wearing a collar, and did not seem well cared for; he was also not neutered. After picking him up, I returned to the car and held him in my lap as we discussed what to do. Evan walked door to door with the dog, and when no one was home, he looked for holes in fences or open gates where this dog may have come from. He walked with him on a leash (a spare from our car) in the hopes that he would lead them back to where he came from, but he just kept veering back to the road.

After an hour with no luck, we brought the dog to the nearby animal center where they looked for a chip but didn't find one. They said they would keep him for forty-eight hours and then send him to a more permanent shelter. We told them if no one showed up we would come back and try the neighborhood again.

The next day we called the center and they informed us he had just been picked up. We were relieved, but also slightly disappointed. It would have been difficult to accommodate a new dog, and we wanted him to find his home; given the condition in which we found him, however, we worried about his situation.

This entire trip and our subsequent return home has become a particularly exhausting memory. While these scenarios are somewhat common occurrences for us, a few difficult moments back-to-back were tiring. I don't know if we acted appropriately in each situation, and it seems that in each there was more to be done. I feel on the fence about all of it, in fact, and question whether my actions were more harmful than helpful. Often the argument against intervening is based on the fact that it's not letting nature take its course—we are taught that we should not intervene, because doing so could cause more harm than good. Certainly, it can be argued that intervening is an emotional act, devoid of logic; the average person has no idea what to do with regard to aiding animals, specifically wildlife, so it's better just to call a professional. But what is to be done when a professional can't be reached, or if they are hours away?

It can equally be argued that we have already intervened, for in each of these situations (mortally wounded chicken and neglected dog) humans are the root cause. When an animal gets hit by a car or a bird flies into a window, that is also our fault, however indirect it may seem. It's okay to look for ways to lessen the suffering. Further intervention in the aftermath of these situations is still letting nature take its course. Humans are of course part of nature too, so I suppose there is an argument for saying we should live our life however we please, regardless of the impact on the non-human animals, because whatever we do is technically natural. Are we not just like the lion at the top of the food chain?

But our disconnection from the land and the creatures we share it with is more of a recent development in terms of human evolution. To ignore the natural world, focusing only on human-centered issues, is a modern behavior. And unlike the lion, we hunt en masse across the entire world. Shouldn't our type of intelligence aid us in making decisions that best serve the planet which in turn, serves us?

* * *

Robin Wall Kimmerer is a scientist, writer, and enrolled member of the Citizen Potawatomi Nation. Her 2013 book *Braiding Sweetgrass* is a collection of autobiographical essays blending indigenous history, traditional ecological knowledge, spirituality, and Western science.[10] Kimmerer opens her essay "Collateral Damage" by envisioning the life of someone in a war zone, as she listens to news reports of bombings and their resulting "collateral damage." Kimmerer contemplates the usage of this term and its real meaning—man-made death and destruction. Eventually, she turns off the radio and leaves home in the middle of a stormy night to carry salamanders across a busy road with fellow volunteers.

Along with other amphibians, these salamanders are returning home from their winter resting spots to the vernal pools of spring, where they will meet their mates and lay eggs. The darkness and the rain allow them to glide more easily to their destination without the risk of drying out. However, a busy road now separates these two locations, and they must make the harrowing journey across this dangerous barrier. The volunteers race to carry as many salamanders across the road as possible before car lights appear over the hill, forcing them to halt their efforts until the traffic passes. Despite the best efforts of the volunteers, the car will likely run over several salamanders in the process; even the vibrations from a passing car can kill this sensitive creature. Kimmerer watches as a car approaches, expecting it to slow down at the sight of their group standing on the shoulder; perhaps the driver will even roll down a window to check that all is well. However, the car hardly brakes before speeding off again, which raises the question: "If cars scarcely brake for *Homo sapiens*, what hope can we hold for *Ambystoma maculata*, our other neighbors who travel this road in the night?" Kimmerer's words remind me of those of Carl Sagan. In his 1973 book *The Cosmic Connection*, Sagan questions whether we could ever truly have a profound respect for all human beings while, at the same time, we ignore all of the other organisms that have evolved alongside us for over 4.5 billion years. "If we survive these perilous times," he states, "it is clear that even an identification with all of mankind is not the ultimate desirable identification."[11]

Students from the university also show up to the salamander crossing that night. Rather than carrying them across, though, they're conducting an assessment for a conservation project at the university—counting how many salamanders make it on their own, and how many are killed by cars. They are hoping to convince the highway department to install culverts for the salamanders so that they can cross without having to use the road. The students apply the data to show how many salamanders are killed before completing their life cycle in the hopes of making a more convincing argument. This project presents an ethical dilemma: the students must not interfere; they can only watch, even as some of the individuals in front of them become collateral damage. Kimmerer acknowledges that she and the other volunteers are skewing that data by saving some of the salamanders, potentially causing more harm than good, but she is unwilling to let the creatures in front of her die. Even the biologist who is leading the university project admits to her that he sometimes is unable to sleep, and travels to the area late at night to help the salamanders cross.

Kimmerer identifies the salamander as the ultimate "other" that is often considered repulsive to *Homo sapiens*. She argues that by assisting these creatures in their journey, she and the other volunteers are coming face-to-face with their own innate xenophobia—a fear and hatred not only reserved for cold-blooded species, but often for their own. "Each time we rescue slippery, spotted beings we attest to their right to be, to live in the sovereign territory of their own lives." Picking up the salamanders is almost a practice in impartiality. Kimmerer does not consider this act altruistic, because the volunteers gain so much from the experience. By aiding the salamanders, they are developing a relationship with a species that could not be more different from their own while, at the same time, witnessing this incredible tradition. She questions whether we are bound to the salamanders as much as we are bound to each other, and relates the war zone to the road, since the two environments are intertwined by oil and a disregard for life. Listening to the news makes her feel powerless, because she can control neither the bombings nor the speeding cars; yet carrying these salamanders, even for one night, gives her a sense of distancing her name from all this human-made destruction.

Kimmerer expresses her own ecological grief through the feelings of helplessness she experiences at her inability to stop the passing cars. Through action, however, she is able to ease her feelings of grief. By writing about her experience, she is also guiding the reader through these feelings, offering insights on how best to manage such difficult emotions. By making the connection between animals being hit by cars to human casualties in war zones, Kimmerer could invoke the common argument, typically directed at animal rights activists, that people care more about non-human animals than human beings. Given the mass consumption of animal products, and the lack of empathy for the majority of non-human animals, this is of course untrue.

Given her background as a scientist, Kimmerer is able to understand the consequences of a species interrupted. Her skills as a writer allow her to convey the importance of this message in an accessible essay that has the ability to reach a greater audience than most scientific studies. Kimmerer is not stating that a salamander's life is the same as that of a human being; instead, she is speaking more broadly about our interconnectedness and the type of behavior that leads to disrespect of all kinds. From this perspective, a disregard for life, whether toward humans or non-human animals, is still a disregard for life. Regardless of where it's directed, the sentiment and behavior involved do not change. Anyone who spends enough time observing animals will also observe animal abuse, and Kimmerer mentions having watched "two young men kicking a toad between them like a hacky sack." It's difficult for me to imagine these same young men would be sensitive to the plights of others who look different from them, human or non.

Scientific data provides information on the extent of species loss and the consequences of that loss to a particular ecosystem. Scientific data, however, lacks the ability to explain what individual creatures are experiencing. Data also has difficulty explaining how it feels to be a human, a powerless witness in the face of the environmental destruction and the spiritual trauma that will surely follow. The data alone also fails to question the notion of one animal, *Homo sapiens*, deciding the importance of another non-human animal, and whether their life is worth saving, especially when the creatures in question can't speak for themselves.

Paul Ehrlich and Brian Walker's rivet-popper hypothesis compares species in an ecosystem to rivets in an airplane.[12] If you remove a few rivets, you can probably still fly; but if you continue removing them, a wing is eventually going to fall off and the plane is going to crash. What is unknown, however, is how many rivets (species) it takes to hold a plane (ecosystem) together. If all of the removed rivets are specialists—species with a narrow ecological niche—then losing even a few could cause the plane to go down. If, on the other hand, there are enough generalists—species that can live in a wide range of habitats and consume a wide variety of food—and redundants—species that fulfill the same role of another and can take over if one is removed from the ecosystem—then the loss of a certain number of rivets matters less for the stability of the system.

This hypothesis is helpful for a broad understanding of the fragility of ecosystems, and it puts the complicated subject of extinction into perspective; however, it also takes individuals and rates their importance based on the roles they fulfill within an ecosystem. One obvious objection to this hypothesis is that these are individual, sentient beings, and the plants and insects on which they depend—not bolts and rivets in airplane wings. It seems unfair to ask science to be impartial, however, when human beings aren't. We are now at a point where it seems unrealistic to ask for ecological science to be untangled from environmental advocacy: If a scientist's work no longer exists due to human-caused climate change, what does that do to the scientist? I'm certainly not arguing against the scientific process or the need for objectivity. I am only pointing out the importance of having more scientists like Kimmerer who are able to decipher the data while looking beyond it to convey its meaning to a wider audience. I'm not sure if Kimmerer's essay has inspired people to leave their homes in the middle of the night to carry salamanders across the road—yet I imagine that it has encouraged readers to reflect on what might have been their own unconscious xenophobia and speciesism. Or, at the very least, it led them to consider the creatures that might be sharing the road at night.

In her TED Talk titled "Why Animal Rights Is Not a Luxury," Rubaiya Ahmad addresses the issue of selective compassion by comparing the traits of her two-year-old son to the cognitive skills of dogs.[13] The talk is primarily focused on the rabies problem in Bangladesh, as well as her proposed solution for it, but she consistently highlights the power that humans have over animals, and how the treatment of animals can make or break a society. Using examples of those typically considered vulnerable by society to highlight the true vulnerability of animals, she speaks about the abilities of a two-year-old to drown a kitten, a "battered housewife" to pour boiling water on a cat, and an elderly person to beat a dog. While the level of control over one's self is certainly situational, it does not seem outlandish to ask how things might be different if self-restraint toward the lives of others, especially non-human animals, was a more commonplace conversation.

As individuals, we seem to have so little control over the world; as a whole, however, we are able to push it to the point of utter destruction. The results of decades of negligence and greed are just now beginning to show, a fact that only serves to amplify feelings of helplessness. I often count on research to give me a sense of control, even if it ultimately proves to be illusory. It's similar to suffering from an unknown illness and obtaining a proper diagnosis, for even if the diagnosis doesn't change the outcome, at least it has a name. On the other hand, perhaps embracing the unknowns of climate change and the lack of control outside our own actions could illicit a new kind of comfort. We are aware to some extent where things are headed, and that we have acted too late and the deadline has passed. In some ways, this brings me relief. The timer is counting down, and the focus can now shift from diffusing the bomb to softening the blow. History shows that our fixation on control—whether over other humans, animals, land, resources, or narratives—constitutes a major part of how we arrived at this capitalist-fueled climate crisis. This fixation on control is also how conservation groups behave as oligarchs, storming into communities they don't belong to and demanding that people adopt a new standard of behavior—conveniently disregarding all the destructive steps it took for their own culture to get to a point of authority in the first place.

* * *

Looking back, I don't know if we made the right decision with the hen; but we didn't know what else to do. I question if we collected trash due to the guilt of being tourists at a neighborhood beach. If we felt that way, why did we go there in the first place? And why did we wait until the last day to clean—why didn't we do it every day? Back home in Texas, should we have left the dog alone? Would he have eventually found his way home, and in our actions we only succeeded in causing more stress for ourselves, the dog, and the dog's caretakers? But what if he got hit by a car? Or mated with another dog while loose? Or hurt another animal? Should we have just kept the dog because of his perceived unhealthy condition, and his lack of identification? I don't have concrete answers for any of it and likely never will, which is often the case when it comes to intervening.

I recently came across an Australian wildlife guide that teaches the practice of pouch checking. It encourages people to stop when they see a kangaroo, echidna, wombat, and other animals on the side of the road, first to check if they are alive, and then to check their pouch (if they have one) for a joey. When kangaroos and other animals with pouches are hit by cars, often the joey survives but subsequently starves to death in their mother's pouch.

The document depicts a visual list of basic items to keep in the car for safely checking pouches, as well as different items like socks and beanies that could be used as a makeshift pouch until the joey is able to receive care. The guide also contains detailed images of the various types of animals and what their pouches look like, as well as the various stages of the joeys. Removal may be different based on the age of the young, and in some cases, it requires the joey to be cut from the mother. It also contains information on rescuing other injured or orphaned wildlife, as well as a number to call where someone will talk you through the various procedures. If an animal is dead and the pouch has been checked, people are instructed to mark the animal on the road with spray paint.

While I know these guides are available in the U.S. through sources like PETA, I cannot imagine that this is practiced with any regularity. Opossums, for instance, are the only marsupial found in the United States; they are not exactly held in high regard. The idea of stopping to check the pouch of an opossum on the side of the road is almost unheard of. This sort of devotion to helping common, local animals in various stages of injury is not a part of American culture, and the practice of keeping items in the car for that specific task would be unimaginable for the majority of citizens. Yet this sort of practice can help emphasize not only individual behavior, but that of entire communities, empowering a shared belief in the responsibility to our non-human neighbors. It grants breathing room for more citizen scientists, rather than keeping knowledge of ecological practices confined to a select few. This may be considered a radical approach to conservation in America even though it should be inherent in a social species such as our own. Helping a creature in pain, regardless of species or their place on the endangered species list, seems like a good starting point.

On that day in Kauai and on my return to Austin, all I could do was react to what was presented to me in those moments, and respond in a way that I perceived to be the most responsible. It's quite rare we find ourselves in extreme or dramatic situations where helping is the obvious thing to do. Most of the time it's not someone falling through the ice or getting stuck on a subway track—most of the time it's a lost or injured animal, or trash on a beach, or salamanders trying to cross the road at night.

Perhaps by helping the salamanders across the road, Kimmerer was slightly altering the data for the university students and prolonging the application of more long-term solutions. I have gone through phases where this type of thinking has caused complete inaction on my part for fear of doing the wrong thing. But I remind myself that I have only felt *true* guilt about the times I didn't try to help, regardless of the outcome—the times that I ignored, or failed to acknowledge, my perceived responsibility. While I was not in control of the initial problem, I was able to affect the aftermath with my personal actions. In the case of the hen, I was able to develop a deeper connection to a species I hadn't previously thought much about. Like Kimmerer, these small interventions allowed me to briefly strike my name from the record, or at least partially undo some of the damage perpetrated by my species.

At Least We Tried

Shopping Won't
Save the World

When it comes to conversations on climate change—especially in American media—there seem to be two dominant narratives. The first could be categorized as technocratic: Focusing primarily on climate solutions, such as decarbonization, with a complete disregard for the broader societal context, it claims to hold all of the answers in its requirement for sweeping changes, yet none of the proposed solutions seem realistic within a time frame that would negate real disaster. With the technocratic approach, the expert explains to the masses what is wrong and how they or their massive corporation alone have the ability to solve it. I associate this kind of thinking with tech bro culture. The term "tech bro" evolved from the concept of a boys' club and has become widespread through internet memes that mock the overwhelmingly male college graduates who dominate the tech space in Silicon Valley in pursuit of the next Google. These approaches often command such a suspension of disbelief as to ignore the injustices of the past and much of human history and behavior in order to be successful. While this culture may have been created by an elite few, it has become widespread; it is also the reason for articles and books with hyperbolic titles, typically a noun followed by, "and How It Transformed the World," or similar embellishments. If this way of thinking were a single person, they would most definitely be into CrossFit, microdosing, and referring to themselves as an entrepreneur, disrupter, and/or changemaker.

The second dominant narrative is apocalyptic. Centering around the *lack* of solution, it suggests that we are simply hurtling further and further into the abyss with each untimely wildfire. This narrative is most prominent on social media. *Look at this charred kangaroo*, it screams at us. *Look at these people climbing off their roofs into boats*. It is consumed by anger and outrage. It seems that this narrative has coalesced more from the left and younger progressives, fed up with the lack of government action regarding climate change. It is difficult for me not to be in this group, as it certainly feels more informed than the former.

However, I don't find either of these two narratives—the technocratic or the apocalyptic—to be particularly helpful, at least not on their own. It seems the technocratic approach gives people a false sense of confidence that some future genius out of Silicon Valley will save us all. Perhaps that will be the case. However, I worry that this idea, that scientists, engineers, entrepreneurs, and AI will fix everything, releases the individual from responsibility, and enables them to maintain their current lifestyle of consuming with abandon—as long as they buy whatever the newest "eco-friendly" product might be, or support brands that promise to plant a tree with every purchase. I worry that it encourages detachment, potentially leading to societal stagnation and a failure to implement positive individual behavioral changes, other than buying a Tesla and voting in presidential elections. Regardless of the outcome of the climate crisis, I would hope that its existence alone would drive changes in behavior and a revaluation of one's own lifestyle and consumer choices.

The apocalyptic narrative tends to encourage outrage, which, in my case, only leads to despair followed by apathy. Why bother trying if it's already over? The most common, flippant conversation among my peers generally goes something like this: "The earth is better without us (humans); hopefully we'll go extinct sooner rather than later so the earth can recover." I should note that I've only heard this sentiment from acquaintances who are unlikely to become climate refugees, or from those without children who have no plans to procreate. It is also most certainly a bluff, as no one would be happy in the face of climate wars, mass migration, disease, and death due to climate change. They are imagining a future long after their lifetime, and it's likely a form of dissociation in an attempt to avoid feelings of grief. In one sense, it's much the same sentiment as "we get the government we deserve."

In her essay "Maple Nation: A Citizenship Guide," from her book *Braiding Sweetgrass*, Kimmerer explains that this mindset ignores the other citizens of our planet who certainly don't deserve the fate humans have created.[14] She speaks specifically of the Maples, whom she refers to as "the standing people," and all that they contribute year-round to the community without ever being asked. "They deserve you and me speaking up on their behalf," she argues.

The narrative that humans should just give up trying, and that we deserve climate change, is clearly harmful and misguided, and it ignores all the suffering for other non-human beings between now and our future extinction. It also misses how intertwined we are with the natural world, and how, in many cases, humans are the reason that much of it still exists. If humans were to go extinct tomorrow, much of life on earth would suffer a tremendous, if temporary, impact.

The apocalyptic mindset shares similarities with the technocratic approach, as both encourage the individual not to change their behavior. Both remove the individual erroneously from being either a positive or negative connection to the climate crisis. In an almost infantilizing way, both narratives relieve citizens of responsibility. We, the perceived innocents, can complain about climate change and the corporations that contribute to it, while still buying from those corporations. After all, it's their fault for making us dependent on them. An example of this perspective would be self-identifying as a progressive, one who relentlessly complains about the existence of billionaires, while simultaneously ordering products from Amazon. While neoliberalism, an ideology that favors free-market capitalism and deregulation, may be at fault for allowing the possibility of infinite wealth, it is consumers who transform that possibility into a reality.

Megan Garber touched on the popularity of nature themes in American consumerism in an article for *The Atlantic* titled "The Dark Side of the Houseplant Boom."[15] She quotes Genesis 1:28— "Fill the earth and subdue it. Have dominion over the fish of the sea, the birds of the air, and all the living things that move upon the earth"—and wonders if this idea has transcended Judeo-Christian belief and infiltrated broader human culture, presenting the earth as a resource rather than a home. She questions whether the millennial obsession with houseplants is a way to ease some of the unconscious guilt and grief about the state of the planet through nursing seedlings into fully grown plants. It's not unreasonable, however, to assume a more sinister element at play, albeit an unconscious one. The collection of houseplants, earth tones, and natural fibers feels like an outward expression of self-exclusion from the climate crisis. It signals a certain educational status, and an awareness that having too much is problematic both as an individual and as a society. But this "simplifying" and minimalist décor feels like yet another form of acquiring nature while simultaneously fetishizing a humbler existence. It would be incorrect of me to assume simplifying one's life is inherently inauthentic, since there are certainly those who choose to live with less and take the endeavor seriously. However, the increasing popularity of decluttering and organizing lacks depth and appears to come from a place of extreme privilege.

Getting rid of everything that doesn't "spark joy" in order to achieve aesthetic gratification, to borrow the Marie Kondo method, isn't encouraging awareness of the culture that made having this much stuff acceptable in the first place.[16] This style of simplifying appears wasteful—more concerned with a perceived awareness rather than a genuine reevaluation of one's own needs and consumerist behavior. Many of the people participating in this minimalist aesthetic will simply repurchase items when the trend grows tired.

The commercialization of nature in the theme of earth tones and woodland-themed baby nurseries is reminiscent of the greenwashing in the early aughts in which it seemed every household item was marketed with overblown claims of being "natural." It is the same type of marketing strategy that allows companies to profit from the public's anxiety about the planet while, at the same time, allowing the consumer to continue acquiring objects. Now, however, the consumer can experience less guilt because these items are organic, regenerative, and recycled. It's difficult not to buy into this form of branding your way out of climate change when there are few other answers available.

It's culturally acceptable for millennials and Gen Z to place blame on previous generations for climate change, but this does not quite stand up to scrutiny. As a whole, yes, the systems that were put in place by older generations certainly screwed over the majority of citizens. Mass production began in the 1920s, and corporations past and present placed capital ahead of a healthy planet. On the other hand, the majority of individuals consumed far less historically than they do now. Like many from her generation, my grandmother will use a single plastic bag for years. She rinses them and lets them dry on her dish rack. If she buys anything from the grocery store in a plastic container, it is used for food storage in her house indefinitely, or, if it starts to become too worn, it will go on to hold loose screws or rubber bands. This has nothing to do with sustainability or climate change; rather, a habit likely formed during World War II rationing. Why would she throw something away that can still be used? Why would she buy something she doesn't need? The term "single-use plastic" is not in her vocabulary. I have never spoken to my grandmother about climate change and, to be honest, given her location, age, and her community, she would likely be a climate change denier. Yet her impact is so minuscule compared to even the most outspoken climate activist—she has even worn the same clothing since the mid-1980s. I once poured myself a second cup of coffee and she talked about it for my entire visit; she couldn't believe I had two coffees. She would be amazed to learn that people order things from online stores and expect them to arrive the same day and are frustrated when it takes longer than two, or that there are massive fast-fashion chains where people buy clothing expecting it to fall apart after a couple of washes. People are buying more things than ever before. If previous generations are to blame for setting the wheels in motion, younger generations are certainly to blame for running it off the rails.

To borrow from Julie Livingston's parable, you can't fight the "self-devouring growth" of capitalism with more capitalism.[17] A system that is inherently anti-intellectual, free-market capitalism robs us of personal enlightenment, pushing us to search for meaning only within its framework, where no meaning can actually exist. Buying "better" products gives one a false sense of being productive, but ultimately leads to dissatisfaction. While it is a positive development that there is an ever-growing list of companies that place their values front and center, and who are equally transparent about materials and employee wages, consumption is still consumption. While a laudable improvement, transparency is still a marketing ploy that primarily benefits the companies themselves. Buying more items because they are marketed as sustainable or carbon neutral falls back on the same flawed logic of getting to eat more of something because it is marketed as having less sugar or fewer calories. Civilization has always depended on self-deception to function, and we must ask what would happen if consumers stopped feeding the market.

When I was at a low point in my illness I began to experiment with food and lifestyle changes in an effort to ease some of my symptoms with the hope that I could eventually stop my vomiting episodes altogether. I prioritized rest, especially around my menstrual cycle. I tried to eat more whole foods and to avoid oils and stabilizers in packaged foods. Social media stressed me out, so I deleted it. Because my illness was such a mystery at the time, a lot of these decisions were based on how my body reacted to each change. I often heard people say things like, "Wow, you are so disciplined. I could never give up [whatever I was abstaining from at the moment]." These observations from others were sometimes said as a compliment and sometimes as an insult, but I found both utterly bizarre. Whenever I had the option not to participate in a behavior that my body was too sensitive to handle, I took it. I had a completely different perspective: for me, it didn't feel like "discipline"; it felt like survival. I was afraid and trying my best not to end up in a dangerous situation, so going to bed early or not consuming certain things didn't really seem like much of a sacrifice for what I received in return, which was staying out of the hospital.

While it may seem overly simple, it has helped me to apply this logic to the climate crisis. My home is sick, so sick that everything I love may not be able to live in it for much longer. I may only be one cell in the body of the earth, but I can at least try to be a good cell instead of a cancerous one. This perspective shift makes the decision to not purchase convenient but needless items a much easier one.

Most U.S. consumers likely understand that the most sustainable item is the one they already own, but it's much easier to just go with the flow of the capitalist river, allowing oneself to believe that the fleeting joy these new products bring outweigh the harm caused in their production. But viewing the earth and its non-human inhabitants as a resource for one's personal enjoyment is what I suppose Americans mean when they speak of "freedom."

Thank You for Shopping

Completely Fresh

Natural Wonders

You Can't Return
If You Never Left

Since the 2020 release of the successful Netflix film *My Octopus Teacher*, there have been numerous debates about the merits of octopuses and how we as humans should be treating them.[18]

The film is primarily about the South African filmmaker and naturalist Craig Foster developing a relationship with a female octopus. Foster inserts himself into the world of the octopus and is set on befriending her rather than observing her from afar. He doesn't wear a wetsuit because he wants as few barriers between him and his surroundings as possible. Over time the octopus begins to trust him and becomes what he believes to be a mentor, allowing him to follow and learn from her behavior. During one of his last interactions with her, she is splayed across his chest in what looks like a hug. Rather than placing the octopus at the center of this story, however, Foster is initially more focused on what she can help him achieve in his own life, and his presence actually puts her in danger at times.

Since this film's release, I have heard numerous people—from my classmates to close friends and family, to characters in films and pop culture podcast hosts—declare that they will no longer eat octopus. They state that the octopus is "too intelligent" and they can no longer imagine eating them; they now feel a kinship and love toward this creature that they didn't exhibit before.

While this research is certainly anecdotal, I presume that upon seeing this in-depth relationship between a human and a cephalopod, many viewers were able to imagine the possibility of interspecies friendships that extend beyond common household pets. At first these declarations of new-found morality and restraint elicited confusion from me. Did any of these people regularly consume octopus in the first place? Yes, the octopus trade is a billion-dollar industry; but compared to the consumption of chicken, it doesn't even come close. It just didn't seem like much of a conviction to me. It reminded me of when I was a kid and I first learned about Lent. I wanted to participate because my friends practiced it, but I had zero context or knowledge of what it was for, so I gave up candy for forty days. I felt so proud of myself even though I didn't really have much access to candy in the first place, so forty days without it was not an unusual occurrence. Regardless of whether or not consuming octopus is actually a reality in their lives or not, their intense love for this species was intriguing. While it's certainly pleasing to hear that the consumption of one species might be on the decline, I also worry that it made octopuses even more popular in home aquariums. This devotion to octopuses also brought to mind all of the other species that would certainly be deemed too intelligent to consume if only a heartfelt documentary were made about them.

I felt these viewers were missing the point of the film entirely and their response was an immediate, superficial reaction to a heartfelt story directly in front of them; it did not develop from a deeper level of understanding, which would then extend to other species aside from the octopus. A more developed understanding of why one should abstain from eating animals is also required for this type of conviction to last; it can't simply be reserved for one species or come from a fleeting moment of sentimentality, or seeing a specific creature as cute or intelligent or more loveable than another.

Foster narrates his story using footage he took while visiting the octopus every day for over a year. He approaches his storytelling from a vulnerable place, and speaks about his exhaustion and frustration with his life and his role as a father. Although Foster is not American, his concerns are familiar to many in the United States. He is overworked and feels drained by the lack of time spent in nature and with his family.

Foster touches on the sadness he feels as an outsider to nature; he understands that he is removed by living in the modern world, and that this is unnatural for human beings. At times he almost evangelizes the idea of the *wild* and *nature*, and praises tracking methods used by hunters in Botswana, which he employs to find the octopus after she flees from him. His hunting tactics to find the octopus, though clearly used to simply find and observe her, still feel rather threatening and make the scenes unsettling to watch. There is also an emphasis on the octopus's intelligence and her own skilled hunting techniques, and how she is able to outwit her opponents. This fascination with a few limited types of intelligence viewed through the human lens tends to favor not only intelligence we recognize in ourselves but also what we seek to achieve in our own lives.

Foster becomes emotional as he recounts a chase between the octopus and a pyjama shark that leaves her injured and weak. He agonizes over whether he should have intervened. He ultimately decides not to interfere, due to the unease that he feels over possibly interrupting "nature's course." He also recognizes the hypocrisy inherent in this, considering that he's developed a friendship with the octopus and she potentially left her den solely to see him, which then put her in danger. Perhaps his presence gave her a false sense of security, which placed her in a vulnerable position. Foster does not view the acclimatization of the octopus with a human as a concern; if anything, he is extremely flattered that she remembers him and seeks him out. Her safety and well-being only seem to occur to Foster after she has been injured. While he decides not to intervene during the shark chase, he can't help but bring her food when she is weak and recovering in her den. The octopus goes on to grow another tentacle in the place of the one she lost to the shark, and eventually she mates with another octopus, an indication that her life is coming to an end. Through tear-filled eyes, Foster remembers the last encounter with his friend, and earnestly describes how much she changed his life. Through his relationship with the octopus, he believes he has become a better person.

Had the film been about his relationship with a pyjama shark, the predator of the octopus, the audience would certainly be rooting for the shark. The scene where the shark attacks the octopus, biting off a tentacle, would find its somber music replaced by something more thrilling or perhaps triumphant, as when the octopus displays her hunting skills. Whenever pyjama sharks are on the screen, the music becomes tense and ominous. Considering the negativity surrounding sharks of all kinds, I found this very disappointing. It seemed to only reinforce the idea that sharks are to be feared and reviled. Creating a villain out of pyjama sharks was clearly done in an effort to create drama and a compelling story. However, I wish Foster recognized that humans would have better filled that role, as we are clearly the biggest threat to both octopuses and sharks.

In the end, Foster does touch on this dissonance; he recognizes that he has viewed creatures as the "other" and that through this relationship he has become "sensitized" to the lives of all creatures.

Indeed, the film later includes footage of a baby pyjama shark being born in an effort to rectify the film's earlier narrative. Foster's use of the word "sensitized" here is noteworthy. "Desensitized" is widely used in our increasingly overstimulated culture, but rarely is "sensitized" used, especially regarding non-human animals. For the majority of us who will never have the opportunity to befriend an octopus or observe a species in its natural habitat for years at a time, how can we become sensitized to them? Is secondhand intimacy enough? Foster didn't seek out the octopus for the betterment of the creature, or to teach the world about the importance of octopuses. He sought out an experience for the betterment of himself alone, and his goal evolved into something bigger through his relationship with the octopus. This idea of returning to nature to find oneself is a popular trope in western culture and sometimes feels reminiscent of John Muir, who preached that "civilized" people must visit nature in order to recharge or find themselves:

> Nowhere will you see the majestic operations of nature more clearly revealed beside the frailest, most gentle and peaceful things. Nearly all the park is a profound solitude. Yet it is full of charming company, full of God's thoughts, a place of peace and safety amid the most exalted grandeur and eager enthusiastic action, a new song, a place of beginnings abounding in first lessons on life, mountain-building, eternal, invincible, unbreakable order; with sermons in stones, storms, trees, flowers, and animals brimful of humanity.[19]

By defining nature as an elixir and preaching wilderness as a pristine temple, untouched by human hands, Muir aided in furthering the divide between human and nature that perhaps did not exist in the United States before the removal of (indigenous) humans so that other (European) humans could explore nature as tourists. To Muir, nature was the closest one could get to God; yet those living within it were considered dirty and less than human.[20] It seems that nature was not meant to be part of one's daily existence; rather, it was an antidote to modern city life. This perceived separation between nature and daily life has had lasting effects on culture, and consequently the planet, with nature itself being seen as the "other."

It's easier to care about an octopus or, indeed, any species, when doing so does not change anything about one's current lifestyle. Are elephants, tigers, rhinos, and polar bears so popular in American culture because they do not exist outside of cages here, and therefore hold our attention? Or is it because we don't like to eat them? It's much easier to convince someone to buy a cute stuffed animal at the zoo with a label stating that doing so supports conservation, than it is to convince them to give up their current lifestyle.

At times, nature documentaries in the style of *Planet Earth* feel alienating, in that most of the viewers will never see a lion hunt a gazelle in person, and it is forever a slow-motion, cinematic event held in the mind.[21] When this tradition ceases, it will be relayed through multiple, distant sources—it will not be experienced or felt beyond the borders of its existence. These films about wildlife that come with a message about the need for conservation feel empty to me and sometimes fall into the trap of depicting nature as the precious other. I can't always tell what the message of these films are. Are they meant to educate? Serve as travel inspiration? Or are they just a historical record of what will soon be gone? A voiceover about the need to take care of our planet often plays over drone footage of picturesque landscapes of elephants, penguins, and lions. The issue with this approach, in my opinion, is that it further creates a separation in the viewer's mind. When nature—or "wild places," as they are often called in these films—is only shown as epic or grandiose, it makes the nature right in front of us become invisible. These films sometimes deepen my grief by highlighting the magnitude of the issue and only glorifying the places and creatures we are quickly losing, ones far away from me, continuously reminding us to help and care—yet without guidance about how to do so. These places are magnificent and should be viewed as such, but I also worry they inform the viewer that nature equals remote, awe-inspiring landscapes and little else. I wish there were more documentaries in the style (and with the budget) of *Planet Earth* that highlighted urban ecology and the nature we so often take for granted, the nature we as individuals could actually positively impact. When an animal crosses the road in a national park, cars all slow to a stop, and some people will even get out of their cars in an attempt to photograph the animals. Yet when an animal crosses the road at home, a different consequence often takes place.

This scenario happened recently on a busy street by the river. I was with my partner, Evan, when we saw a turtle making its way across the street in an attempt to reach the riverbank. The turtle was large enough to see from afar, yet the cars in front of us veered around it. We pulled the car over to the side of the road, and Evan got out to retrieve the turtle. The cars failed to stop even for Evan; he had to wait for a break in traffic to retrieve the turtle and return them to the riverbank.

Often narratives around climate change tell us that nature does not exist on the side of the road. Nature is not opossums, snails, raccoons, or salamanders. Nature is not a garden, yard or an alley. If more narratives presented it as such, I imagine more people would have stopped or at least slowed down for the turtle.

Compared to the usual mascots of climate change, a common turtle is not perceived as noteworthy or important. This proves to me why charismatic megafauna and icebergs are not the most productive images to use when promoting awareness on this crisis. I understand why an iceberg is so often used; aside from being a metaphor—the problem of climate change is a much bigger problem than we can see from the surface—it also represents the melting of the glaciers. The iceberg is also striking and big, just like the polar bear and the rhino. We do not typically come across icebergs in the United States, so they catch our attention more than, say, *Doryopteris angelica*, an endangered fern native to Kauai, or the ocelot, a wild cat native to the southwestern U.S. While I understand the need to catch one's attention in an environment of continually shrinking attention spans, this imagery isn't helpful, and, in some ways, promotes the idea of selectively caring about the environment. How does one stop poachers on a different continent from killing rhinos? The emphasis seems often to be placed not on individual behavior, but instead more on grand gestures or infrequent actions like donations and voting. One can choose to either be a scientist or travel across the world to participate in once-in-a-lifetime voluntourism expeditions that are likely detrimental and create a false sense of productivity. Solely promoting these actions only reinforces the idea that we are somehow separate from nature, and can dip in and out when we want to help, rather than acknowledging that nature is all around us and nothing is untouched by human hands, however uncomfortable that may feel.

When one makes climate action a chore or a habit, however, it becomes another aspect of life—albeit an often boring one. While this falls somewhat into the mindset of "think globally, act locally," it is more about creating a standard of behavior for oneself that transcends location, and perhaps embraces the chore of responsibility without the expectation of a result.

In her TED Talk "Nature Is Everywhere," Emma Marris speaks about the places we consider to be the most remote or the wildest—"places that we think of as kind of Edenic representations of a nature before we screwed everything up."[22] She further explains how "even these Edens are deeply influenced by humans." She uses North America in her example:

> About 15,000 years ago when people first came here, they started a process of interacting with the nature that led to the extinction of a big slew of large-bodied animals, from the mastodon to the giant ground sloth, saber-tooth cats, all of these cool animals that unfortunately are no longer with us. And when those animals went extinct, the ecosystems didn't stand still. Massive ripple effects changed grasslands into forests, changed the composition of forests from one tree to another. So even in these Edens, even in these perfect-looking places that seem to remind us of a past before humans, we're essentially looking at a humanized landscape.

The injured animal in front of us is as much a part of nature as the polar bear across the world we so desperately want to save. If one's behavior is to not help unless it is a scheduled activity, or thought of as something to do somewhere else, why would that behavior change in a different set of circumstances? If someone can't even help a turtle get across a road, what makes them think they would be of any use when a larger crisis occurs?

The problem of climate change is that it is simply too large. It is almost impossible to put it in perspective. Trying to come up with definitive solutions feels almost comical. In some ways the undertaking reminds me of that cliché about writing—that it's viewed as too precious, and although many people may dream of becoming authors, it's often thought of as some far-off future achievement. The process of book-writing is often placed on a pedestal; it's something that requires a year in a secluded cabin with a desk facing a pond, an impossible situation for most. With this mindset, it is very unlikely that the individual will write the book, because the dream is so specific and difficult to obtain. Most writers have lives that require much of their attention to be spent elsewhere, and they understand writing to be a daily habit or even a chore. I presume more writing gets done during subway commutes, and in the hours before and after work, than in idyllic countryside cottages. It's the dilemma mentioned in the introduction—the one in which I often find myself. Nature is precious. Writing is precious. And both feel just out of reach, inhabiting a pedestal in the mind. They can't just be like every other chore on any other day—yet that is exactly what they are.

What I find so effective about storytellers like Robin Wall Kimmerer, Hope Ryden, and Elisabeth Tova Bailey is that they highlight the chore of conservation. Kimmerer does not fly to Antarctica with a camera crew for a Netflix special on climate change. She drives to a nearby road in the dark to pick up tiny creatures that most humans never give a second thought. While Ryden's work is certainly harder to achieve in terms of the time she devoted, the beaver dam was still just fifteen minutes from her house, which she cited as a requirement when scouting for animals to observe. Bailey is forced into watching at first, but then that observation becomes an act of love and healing. They spend time observing vulnerable creatures that exist all around us that many will never see, despite having ample opportunity to do so. By observing, they learn *when* and *how* to intervene. They become students of the natural world. Rather than "returning" to nature, they have changed their relationship to it and their behavior within it.

In her book *Rambunctious Garden*, Emma Marris states,

> Yes, nature is carefully managed national parks and vast
> boreal forest and uninhabited arctic. Nature is also the birds
> in your backyard; the bees whizzing down Fifth Avenue
> in Manhattan; the pines in rows in forest plantations;
> the blackberries and butterfly bushes that grow alongside
> the urban river; the Chinese tree-of-heaven or "ghetto
> palm" growing behind the corner store; the quail strutting
> through the farmer's field; the old field overgrown with
> weeds and shrubs and snakes and burrowing mammals;
> the jungle thick with plants labeled "invasive" pests; the
> carefully designed landscape garden; the green roof;
> the highway median; the five-hundred-year-old orchard
> folded into the heart of the Amazon; the avocado tree that
> sprouts in your compost pile. Nature is almost everywhere.
> But wherever it is, there is one thing that nature is not:
> pristine.[23]

Marris understands that nature is everywhere, not just in the
faraway, unreachable places. Western science often teaches us not
to intervene because we may end up causing more harm than good,
yet holding on to this belief so tightly feels an awful lot like gospel.
Being taught that only a select few have the credentials to intervene
also encourages regular citizens not to take responsibility for their
own actions. Perhaps moving beyond this strict doctrine would
allow for more citizen scientists and therefore a more productive
society regarding climate action. Marris states,

> A consequence of throwing out the "pristine wilderness"
> ideal is that conservationists, and society at large, now have

to formulate alternative goals for conservation. This may be in part why we are so reluctant to move on. After all, "putting things back the way they were" seems to handily cover any other goals we might have.

I would also argue that finding value where it could previously be discarded makes life more complicated and requires living in a gray area, which is uncomfortable and requires hard work. Thankfully, we do not live in a black-and-white world, and instead live in a world full of nuance. Perhaps if we can find comfort in our gray reality, we will begin to see the nature that lives here with us.

Perspective

Checklist

How am I expressing grief?
What is my response?
What are my fears?
Do I try to bring a baby into this world?
Evan's question:
"Shouldn't we live our lives and make choices for us? Just because we have the awareness doesn't mean we shouldn't get to experience all aspects of life we want to experience."
But because we know, aren't we obligated to act in response?
But do we actually know anything?
What if everything turns out okay and it was all for nothing?
Meteors I guess, that's something to worry about
What keeps me up at night? The death of everyone I love
Factory farms
Clean air
Nuclear war
Mispronouncing an author's name in 2012
Pompeii
Colonialism
Why do humans think they're so special?

Drew says, "Every generation is so self-absorbed to think that the world is ending and that they can do anything about it. Nothing ever happens."

1957

Lost in Satellites

This past summer I found myself in Marfa, a small town in West Texas, and then in Joshua Tree National Park. I felt a desperation to go to both places after seeing *Villes éteintes* (*Darkened Cities*) by the French artist Thierry Cohen.[24] *Villes éteintes* presents a series of composite images featuring cities illuminated solely by the constellations of the night sky. The images left me queasy: they presented a reality that, aside from some extreme disaster, will never be visible. I often look up at the stars, but my proximity to a downtown area usually limits my field of vision. I had forgotten what it was like to truly *see* stars, and I found the experience of being reminded disheartening. I drove west for a certain reassurance: that the stars I could no longer see at home were indeed still there.

In West Texas there are designated International Dark Sky Places, meaning there are laws protecting the night sky from light pollution. These designated places can be found all over the world, especially in national parks, and I was eager to visit one in the U.S. to calm my anxieties. Outside Marfa, I took several long-exposure images that brought out more stars than I could see with the naked eye, but I also saw several long, straight lines darting all around the images, some red, some white. There were some images where the streaks were very obvious and bright, and others where they were so thin and dim, they looked like a stray hair. These streaks were the paths of satellites. In Joshua Tree, the night sky was even more vibrant, and I could see more of the Milky Way without the aid of a camera. I could also see more satellites.

Only those alive before 1957 were able to view the night sky without the presence of satellites. Thousands have been launched since; currently there are almost 5,000, but by 2030 there may be over 50,000. The United States has more satellites orbiting earth than any other country, with SpaceX, Elon Musk's company, currently owning the most. Satellites are inarguably incredible and disputing their presence is pointless; it would also be naïve, however, to assume that Musk and other private entities are launching thousands of satellites for any purpose beyond profit and the growth of their own corporations.

The vast majority of satellites are used for communication. We use them for the internet, scientific and business purposes, to facilitate consumer transactions, to assist the military, and for navigation. The idea of the night sky *not* being polluted is unrealistic, and my intention is not to romanticize a pre-satellite life. Yet as billionaires continue to compete with one another, and pursue their attempt to colonize space, it is hard not to question their quest for dominion over the sky. If and when spaces such as the night sky that have the ability to connect us to the quieter, more introspective parts of ourselves are no longer accessible, will our connection to our past and our future be affected? That was part of the question that carried me to Marfa. With STEM subjects rapidly replacing the humanities in an effort to secure a more financially viable future, I wondered if context about the inner workings of human beings would be obliterated in the name of "movement"—not progress, I note, because to call it "progress" would be a mistake. Without context there cannot be progress.

The most incredible night sky I have ever witnessed was in New Zealand. It was 2010, and I was backpacking with a friend. We camped along the coast and visited Great Barrier Island. I remember walking along the beach and looking up at the sky. I had been listening to a lot of Bob Dylan at the time, and Mr. Tambourine Man played in my head. There were 997 satellites in space then, but I don't remember any that night—only stars. There were 3,855 more satellites when I visited Joshua Tree last summer, and this time, I noticed.

In Joshua Tree I laid down, just as I had in Marfa, and watched the satellites move through the stars. I thought about Bob Dylan again, and all the other art made with the natural world in mind. For millions of years beings looked to the sky for answers, guidance, navigation, and inspiration. In the Anthropocene, we have created our own stars for essentially the same purpose. I am so appreciative that designated Dark Sky Places exist, but if space itself isn't being protected, what exactly is being preserved? I can't help but question the need for the significant anticipated increase of satellites to the amount currently in space. Will anyone find solace in the stars in 2050 or 2075? Gazing at the perceived stillness, waiting for the occasional falling star will be replaced by constant motion. I wonder if art inspired by the night sky will cease to exist, or if it will simply be inspired by satellites and technology instead.

A study published in 2017 by the Association for Psychological Science about the decline of nature-themed words in pop culture found that from the 1950s there has been a cultural shift away from nature. This has been characterized by a steady decrease of nature-themed words in literature, songs, and films. References to human-made environments have not suffered a similar decrease. Why is this? The study looked at the possible link between the loss of nature-themed words and urbanization as a factor, but concluded that it was "not the only or dominant one." While the study acknowledges the importance of questions such as those that ask whether people think of nature more in terms of practicality rather than spiritualism or aesthetics, it is not able to explain what precisely has happened.

> Cultural products not only reflect the prevailing culture, they also shape it. Books, songs, and films are agents of socialization that help people to form, maintain, and reinforce particular worldviews. The flagging cultural attention to nature means a muting of the message that nature is worth paying attention to and being talked about. It also means a loss of opportunities to awaken curiosity, appreciation, and awe for nature. The loss of physical contact with nature, combined with a parallel loss of symbolic contact through cultural products may set in motion a negative feedback loop, resulting in diminishing levels of interest in and appreciation for nature.[25]

Culturally, we often look to the next generation to move society forward. We imagine children to be better, believe they will somehow care more and be the generation to save us—almost as if there were a sea of Greta Thunbergs just waiting in the wings. And while every generation has brought more progress, what happens when nature-themed words cease to exist in popular culture? I had almost forgotten what a true night sky could look like until an art piece reminded me. What happens when those reminders stop coming?

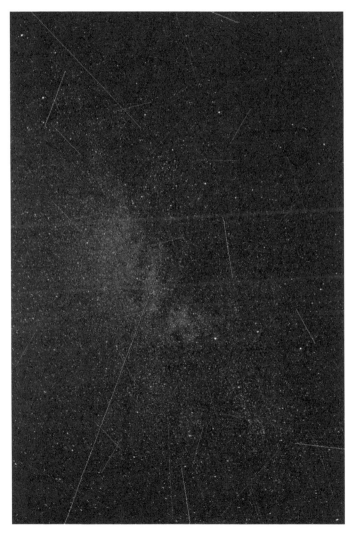

West Texas

An open sky reminiscent of the coast,
but there is no ocean here
Only more sky,
occasionally darkened by rainfall
Low on the horizon behind the still glowing mountain range,
an unexpected storm arrives—has it rained more than usual?
A tarantula darts across the road for more of the same
The wind moves the easter grass together like one green wave,
and blows my shower sideways—hot water stirred with cold air
Inside the windows are fogged but it's an illusion
Clouds burn off by 10 a.m.
It's clear and bright out here.

West Texas

Opting Out

When I was eleven years old, I saw a news story about animal abuse in the circus. Hidden footage showed trainers beating elephants with heavy chains. At the time, it was the most upsetting visual I had ever seen and it brought on thoughts and feelings I hadn't yet experienced. I decided I would never attend a circus. Even if the animals were treated well, it felt deeply unfair that they should have to perform at all. This led me to start questioning the idea of eating animals. Until that news story, I hadn't quite made the connection that the meat on my plate belonged to someone. That I was eating the remains of someone that once had thoughts and feelings. I also began to understand that they were slaughtered because of me, which felt a lot like attending a circus, so I became a vegetarian.

I've been vegan for over eight years now, but up until then I wasn't always a consistent vegetarian. There were even a few years when I ate animals again. Yet the image of that elephant and how it made me feel never left my mind. After becoming a vegan, I questioned how as a vegetarian I could have ever gone back to eating animals after the realization that it was wrong. The only conclusion I've come to is that it must be connected to different ways of knowing. I knew it was wrong, but I didn't *know* it. I had sympathy for non-human animals, but I wasn't yet able to empathize until becoming vegan. When people learn that I am vegan, sometimes they will say something like, "Oh yeah, I was vegan for a few years, but I love bacon too much." I used to find comments like these frustrating because, to me, that kind of reasoning means that they were never a vegan to begin with; it's not something you can stop *knowing*. They may have avoided animal products for a few years because it was good for the environment, or because they "love" animals, or for health reasons, but they were never a vegan. This response no longer frustrates me because I realize that as with many important lessons in life, it often takes learning it several times before it truly sinks in. I've been a vegan for eight years, but I gave up consuming any kind of animal-derived product over nine years ago. Even after a year of living a vegan lifestyle, I still didn't *know* what it actually meant to be a vegan. I'm sure there are many people who are practicing veganism who haven't felt that shift in being. That doesn't mean they won't get there—it only means that until they do, abstaining from animal products is more of a challenge and there is always a chance of abandoning this newfound principle.

The terms plant-based and vegan are often used interchangeably, but they are two different things. When someone says they are vegan "most of the time" or "on weekends," what they mean is that they refrain from eating animal products most of the time through eating a plant-based diet. Plant-based refers to food that does not contain animal ingredients. A food cannot technically be vegan; it can only be vegan-friendly or plant-based. A person who is vegan eats a plant-based diet, but non-vegans can also eat a plant-based diet. Only a person who follows the philosophy of veganism is a vegan. There are also various products that are labeled "vegan-friendly" or "cruelty-free" that shouldn't be, based on the ethics of veganism. An example of such a product is palm oil, which is commonly made using unsustainable production methods. While all palm oil is plant-based, it is widely known to be a major contributor to deforestation in places that contain more biodiversity than anywhere else on earth. Unsustainable palm oil plantations destroy habitats of already endangered species; therefore, in most cases, it should not be considered vegan-friendly even though it is a plant-based product. While these distinctions may seem tedious or irrelevant, they matter.

The Vegan Society defines veganism as "a philosophy and way of living which seeks to exclude—as far as is possible and practicable—all forms of exploitation of, and cruelty to, animals for food, clothing or any other purpose; and by extension, promotes the development and use of animal-free alternatives for the benefit of animals, humans and the environment."[26]

Those who follow this philosophy sometimes refer to themselves as *ethical vegans* as a distinction from those who may follow a plant-based diet for personal health reasons. But I would argue that this philosophy is the only true form of veganism, and that those who follow a plant-based diet only, should refrain from identifying as such. While veganism is not a religion, it does directly affect all of the choices a vegan makes and is an integral part of life. I consider veganism to be as spiritual as it is practical. The definition specifically points to non-human animals because they are being exploited in far greater numbers than any group of humans, and it is humans who are causing this harm. However, the practice of nonviolence and respect certainly extends to all living beings. I would also like to highlight the part of the definition that states "*seeks* to exclude—as far as is *possible* and *practicable.*" I'm under no illusions that my existence is without harm, or that I am free from participating in some form of animal suffering, however far removed it may be.

In his book *Porkopolis*, Alex Blanchette outlines the porcine industrial complex and what it means to use *all* of the pig.[27] He examines the ways in which pigs are "industrially slaughtered and disassembled" into over a thousand products ranging from biodiesel to leather to inkjet paper, and shipped all over the world. Before a piglet is even born, their body is promised to thousands of corporations: "The pig's dead body is in history, with capitalists finding new ways to take it apart." He makes it clear that it is nearly impossible to live in modern society without being in contact with dead pigs in some form or another, and that this fact should matter to us regardless of our beliefs about animal welfare.

> Factory farms effectively turn many of our routine activities into sinks for industrialized biology. This is not usually treated as a political matter, but I would argue that this is a mistake. It should be possible to use the internet, drive down a highway, or have something delivered in a truck without being in contact with porcine particles. Everyday human life in the United States is increasingly lived as a subsidy to industrial meat.

Like many corporations, it seems the goal of the modern meat and dairy industry is to become so deeply intertwined with our lives that they become invisible necessities to us, and we no longer know how to live without them. "What emerges, across sites, is not so much a finished achievement as a fragile and ongoing process that must continually enlist new kinds of consumers to sustain its growth," Blanchette concludes. He suggests this goes far beyond simply resisting meat as a consumer and should extend to every aspect of our lives the meat industry touches. "Rather than simply refusing to eat meat," Blanchette continues, "a basic demand should be the right to remain autonomous from the factory farm—not to be forced to subsidize these operations within our mundane actions."

I drive a car. I use a laptop and a cell phone. I consume electricity. I live in the most destructive country on earth and I have much more than I need. Many areas of my life are destructive—areas where I cannot avoid harming the environment and the creatures living within it. And for Americans who wish to make the argument that China and India create more emissions than the U.S., I would ask that you simply look at where the majority of items in your home are made—it will become quite clear to which place those emissions should be attributed. In terms of the meat industry, Blanchette writes, "Few other countries allow this degree of carnal production density, such that a massive formation of animality cohere that can be treated as akin to environmental deposits for extraction."

Medicine is often tested on animals; vaccines are tested on animals and often have animal components; however, avoiding these things is not always *possible* or *practicable* for me. That doesn't mean I lose the awareness of how these things came to be. It means I somberly accept that which I cannot change and try my best to make up for it in places where change is *possible* and *practicable.* It took me a long time to accept this, and it doesn't mean it doesn't hurt. I have gone through phases where I couldn't accept the idea of causing harm in any way, and I would be overcome with guilt if I received the wrong food order—one containing animal ingredients—or had to take medication that I knew was developed and approved through animal testing. It made me almost completely immobile. When you examine all the ways in which humans cause suffering, it can be overwhelming—and it is difficult not to take it to the extreme. But my real problem was not the indirect harm I was causing; it was that I could not accept reality. The acceptance of reality allows for a shift in focus from what cannot be achieved toward actions that can be controlled.

Veganism is a daily meditation that forces a certain type of consciousness. One may not have the opportunity to literally ease the suffering of those around them on a daily basis, but abstaining from additional violence feels like a good compromise. When friends and family speak to me about veganism, they will say things like, "It seems easy to be vegetarian, but veganism is so extreme." Or they might say, "I could be vegan, but I love cheese too much." Again, they are confusing a diet with a philosophy. If they believed the philosophy, they would no longer want to consume animal products and veganism would no longer look extreme to them. My response is always the same: If vegetarianism seems easier for you, do that. Or if eating a plant-based diet except for cheese is a possibility for you, great, go for it! Despite these "easier" options, there is rarely follow-through.

My observations lead me to believe that Americans tend to feel as though they must be all-or-nothing in whatever endeavor they wish to undertake, which is unfortunate. This mindset obviously lends itself to failure, because it is very difficult to be all-or-nothing with anything in life, especially when it comes to something that isn't a belief system, rather a chore or a diet. I would argue that giving up meat a few days a week because you think it's healthy, or you think you should for the environment and animal welfare, is psychologically much harder than being a vegan. It's difficult to create your own boundaries and measurements when they are not sufficiently reinforced. It's the same mentality as starting something new on a Monday, or on New Year's Day. It's common to slip up, but instead of just continuing on, the desire to either start the clock over or completely give up is often too strong.

It is common to criticize veganism and approaches such as self-control regarding consumerism as being unfair. It is seen as a privileged position to suggest that citizens be held accountable for their lifestyles and behaviors. What about those in poverty, or those who live in food deserts? It's not fair to expect them not to order from Amazon when that is the only option they can afford, or ask them to pass up a fast-food burger when it's that or nothing. I completely agree with this sentiment; however, it is not a relevant argument against veganism or forms of self-control. It's absurd to suggest that someone who is barely surviving should work even harder to survive. That is most likely not *possible* or *practicable*—rather, it should be the obligation of those in more privileged positions to work harder on their neighbor's behalf. In academic circles, the discussion tends to lean into being a voice for the most vulnerable humans in society. It is obviously important for those in positions of privilege to consider those who aren't at the table, but there is an issue when those in power use this argument as a deflection in order to not address their own harmful behavior. Often, the loudest arguments about privilege are coming from those at private universities in large American cities, from those who are not personally faced with food deserts or poverty, and who actually do have the ability to take on more responsibility if they would allow for even the mildest form of discomfort. Arguments about class used by the wealthy are a shield for not allowing the conversation to move forward. They also prevent the argument from becoming personal, which would force introspection on their part.

I never thought I would appear rich for eating rice and beans instead of meat, but this is the dystopian moment we find ourselves in. It should be incredibly disturbing that a burger costs less than an organic apple in some cases. Anger over this should not be directed at vegans; rather, government subsidies that throw money at the meat industry and not produce are to blame. It is ironic that this same government recommends several cups of fruit and vegetables a day to maintain health. Even still, it is certainly possible to create meals from plants for very little money. Before I was a vegan, I ate like one because it was all I could afford. I worked at a bakery for $7.25 an hour and lived in Brooklyn with two roommates. Staples of my shopping list included rice, beans, peanut butter, cabbage, carrots, celery, onions, bananas, melons, and potatoes, most of which can be bought in bulk. Perhaps I could have saved a few cents here and there had I lived off of fast food, but I imagine the medical implications associated with such behavior would outweigh any immediate savings. Even during the times when I consumed animals, I couldn't support a ninety-nine cent burger because I viewed it as an indicator of the factory conditions where that animal came from and the life of the worker who slaughtered them. I've since learned that no dollar amount could justify such atrocities.

While it may not be our fault that corporations and governments are corrupt and they should certainly be held responsible for their actions, this is an irrelevant argument. Governments don't do nearly enough, and corporations are given a pass regarding environmental destruction for the sake of capital; this is the reality in which we live. I would argue that if an individual is frustrated with the lack of effort from their government on the issues they care about, they should act accordingly, regardless of who is elected.

Veganism is often viewed as extreme. I have been told it only serves to make those around me uncomfortable and my own life more difficult. I have been told I am too religious about it, and that it isn't actually doing anything; the impact is so insignificant that it is virtually pointless. I get sent memes about vegans crying or how they are weak and obnoxious. Mocking vegans is a favorite

American pastime, like watching football or talking about cheese; however, in recent years, more awareness on the connection between the climate crisis and the meat and dairy industry has led to campaigns like "Meatless Mondays." While cutting down on meat consumption one day a week is, in many cases, applauded, veganism is still widely thought of as extreme. However, I have observed a more accepting tone in recent years. There is a clear irony in being called extreme for abstaining from animal cruelty, while slaughtering animals en masse is considered normal. I believe most people are genuinely upset by animal cruelty, and vegans serve as a reminder to them that they partake in it. Perhaps being annoyed or uncomfortable is actually a reflection of that inner struggle more so than it is about the vegan at the table. I also care far more about animals and the planet than I do about making someone who doesn't more comfortable.

Ninety-nine percent of meat in the U.S. is factory farmed, but let's pretend for a moment that only the utopian farms depicted on yogurt cups existed. Is there a humane way to kill someone who doesn't want to die? Someone who is happy and healthy? What would that look like exactly? How would it be done?

The dairy industry isn't free from slaughter, either. Cows do not produce milk freely; like human mammals, they produce milk because they become pregnant. Cows in the dairy industry become pregnant through insemination with the use of a device sometimes referred to as a "rape rack." When they give birth, their calf is taken away from them so their milk can be sold to human strangers. If the calf is a male, and therefore of no use to the dairy industry, he becomes what we know as veal. Like humans, cows are incredibly social, and their family life is a fundamental part of their well-being. It is common for the mother to bellow in agony for days after her calf is taken away from her. I find the support of such a gruesome and heartless industry (through the purchase of dairy products) particularly troubling. I also can't help but wonder what ingesting the secretions of a suffering and angry mother does to the spirit of a person. I mention this to say, the reality of these production methods is likely what runs through a vegan's mind when someone is talking about their dependence on cheese.

Returning to the belief of veganism as an extreme practice, it could also be argued that carrying salamanders across a dark road in the rain is extreme, and that the act itself is insignificant to the species—but that would completely disregard the act's significance to the actual salamander whose life is being saved, as well as the significance to Kimmerer's own mental well-being. The term "mutualism" is typically reserved for non-human species that have a symbiotic relationship: while two separate species could live without one another, their relationship benefits them both. Veganism allows humans to enter into mutualistic relationships with countless species and the earth herself. It is as much altruistic as it is a form of self-care. Every choice gives us the opportunity to break away from a long history of dominion and violence. With veganism, every choice is an act of self-control rooted in compassion, and lasts because it holds meaning; it comes from a place of empathy and a desire to ease suffering by refusing to participate wherever possible. It's not a diet that comes with a "cheat day;" it's a belief system built on compassion and resistance.

I once heard someone say, "If you are feeling insecure, just do the right thing," and while that may be an overly simplistic view, it has proven true in my experience. Living in a way that is, for the most part, in step with my values gives me a feeling of strength and confidence that I didn't previously have. It's the same feeling as overcoming an obstacle, except it is built into my daily life. Being aware of every purchase, every ingredient, and every material creates a consciousness around all forms of consumerism that permeates into other areas of life, and allows me to observe nature and my place within it.

It is convenient to believe that world leaders or tech CEOs better understand the issue of climate change and will solve it for the rest of us, but this is not a convincing argument. Furthermore, whether or not the earth is livable for *Homo sapiens* generations from now is somewhat irrelevant to me because I do not have the power to control that, and hoping for it is futile. I accept that we cannot go back to a time when humans were not the dominant force on the planet. I don't believe my mundane chores and daily choices are going to stop the suffering of sentient beings across the world, or fix the climate crisis, but they do shift my relationship to it and help me to cope with the reality of the Anthropocene; they also help me to take responsibility for my part in it. I may only choose how to proceed with what is presented to me in any given moment. By choosing not to participate in unconscious violence and consumerism, I am able to free myself from neoliberal ideology. By choosing to help an injured animal, I am able to ease the physical suffering of the individual in front of me and the mental suffering in myself. However insignificant this may seem; it is the sum of my life.

Forget Your Perfect Offering

Peter Singer is a moral philosopher and a professor of applied ethics. He is best known for his work in the animal rights movement, popularizing the use of the term *speciesism*, and as a proponent of effective altruism through his organization The Life You Can Save. One of his TED Talks, "The Why and How of Effective Altruism," begins by showing the audience graphic footage from a news story in China.[28] A toddler is hit by a car, and the driver stops and rests his back wheel on her for over a second before continuing on. Several people pass by the toddler, almost stepping on her, and another car runs her over before a street cleaner calls for help. By then, however, it is too late. She dies at the hospital.

Singer asks his audience to raise their hand if they think they would have stopped to help the child. Of course, most, if not all, raise their hand. He then cites statistics about the thousands of children dying every day due to poverty and preventable diseases. Then he asks whether that's the same thing. Does it matter that these children are far away, and that the audience can't see them? Isn't not helping these children morally the same thing as walking past the toddler in the street? He considers the two to be morally the same.

Singer explains that we all spend money on things we don't need. Instead, that money could be spent on saving lives around the world through the purchase of items such as mosquito nets. He also compares how much further money can go in developing countries versus in the United States. He uses the example of Sisyphus pushing the boulder up the hill only to have it roll back down again for eternity, and compares this monotonous torture to what he terms the "consumer lifestyle." He explains that this lifestyle of unnecessary purchases will never bring fulfillment or satisfaction. Effective altruism—requiring, in part, giving a set percentage of your income to the most effective charities—is the way to achieve meaning, fulfillment, self-esteem, and a life worth living.

Much of what Singer is trying to achieve here is, in my opinion, valid. Persuading wealthy people to put their money toward more responsible humanitarian efforts, rather than spending it on things they don't need, makes sense. Furthermore, the specific charities and organizations he highlights through The Life You Can Save are, in my opinion, fantastic. On the other hand, the idea that spending money differently will achieve a state of fulfillment for the donor doesn't seem promising.

The graphic and extremely upsetting video in Singer's talk manipulates the audience by first disarming them and then making them feel superior. He elicits feelings of guilt about their own behavior, and when they are in this vulnerable state, he essentially tries to upsell them like a car salesman. Singer's talk comes across as a calculated roller coaster, resulting in whiplash and open wallets.

The problem with effective altruism is that it still fits within the neoliberal framework that ultimately brings dissatisfaction, regardless of where the money is flowing. It also sends a message that one should strive to make as much money as possible in order to give it away—something that Singer actually argues for in the talk. It's no wonder this philosophy is so popular among the bros of Silicon Valley (Sam Bankman-Fried is one of the more infamous examples of the "earning to give" mentality). It also provides a pass for the unrestricted growth of corporations, because, in theory, they help the community by offering more jobs. It reinforces the long-held American belief that riches make you morally superior. The wealthy must have just worked harder than everyone else. The good guy with a gun, the kindly slave owner, the billionaire who uses his wealth for good—it's American mythology reframed and retold generation after generation.

Donating money—especially to charities that are known to be successful—is a wonderful thing to do if you have the means. But the idea that this alone will somehow bring meaning, fulfillment, self-esteem, and "a life worth living" feels a bit unsavory.

The video Singer uses in the beginning of his talk is also an odd choice for proving his point. He is clearly using it to show the horror of people ignoring a suffering child, but it seems to work against his argument, which is that the suffering in front of us is the same as the suffering across the world. While we might ignore suffering outside our immediate field of vision, we would be unlikely to do so if it was directly in front of us. However, what this video actually shows is that people are capable of ignoring suffering even if it is within their field of vision. The video is a better example of the uphill battle of encouraging individual action, in cases where one has the ability to physically do something. If it is this difficult to get someone to take action when there is a critically injured child directly in front of them, why does Singer think people will give money to children across the world that they can't even see? It likely has to do with the ease of donating money directly from your phone, rather than having to become personally involved. But if someone doesn't actively participate, how could this truly be fulfilling?

Long term, these donations likely become automatic monthly withdrawals that are forgotten and discontinued when a card expires. Singer implies that donating money allows someone to break the rut of consumerism, but donating money to a charity does not require problem-solving or any significant behavioral change; it is simply another form of online shopping. The urge to purchase items for oneself does not dissipate when spending money on others. If someone can afford to donate money, it doesn't seem likely that they are choosing one or the other—rather, they are most likely donating in addition to making those unnecessary purchases for themselves. Effective spending won't solve poverty, bring personal fulfillment, or fix the climate crisis if the majority of wealth remains concentrated in a select few. Perhaps this argument is less about persuading Singer's audience to donate and more about peddling the general belief that excessive wealth is a positive as long as the holders of it give some away to the less fortunate.

A more useful interpretation of "the Sisyphus problem" comes from Albert Camus's essay "The Myth of Sisyphus."[29] Camus relates the pushing of the boulder as a metaphor for life and the search for meaning, and views Sisyphus as the absurd hero of the story. Camus describes absurdism as the irrational relationship humans have with the universe: the conflict between the human desire for meaning, and the inability to find it in a chaotic universe. The need for patterns is part of the human condition—it brings a level of comfort because it gives us answers, and this eases the uncertainty of living in a random universe. But the largest challenge *Homo sapiens* are likely to face—climate change—is without a pattern, and we will not find comfort there.

When the images of earth cling too tightly to memory, when the call of happiness becomes too insistent, it happens that melancholy arises in man's heart: this is the rock's victory, this is the rock itself. The boundless grief is too heavy to bear. These are our nights of Gethsemane. But crushing truths perish from being acknowledged.

The annual climate change reports continue to bring sobering projections. That is our reality, and no amount of wishful thinking is going to stop the current trajectory. Based on the previous actions of our own government, as well as governments around the world, there is a lack of motivation and ability to act in a timely manner. Whenever they do succeed in some positive policy, it proves to be a drop in the bucket. It thus seems reasonable to have zero faith in any government's capacity for negating the harmful effects of climate change. Not acting because the severity of the climate crisis is inevitable is the equivalent to giving up on life due to the awareness that life ends. If we do all we can in the hopes of living a healthy life, for as long as possible, should that not extend to our home and those that share it?

Sisyphus is doomed to push the boulder for eternity, but Camus imagines the moment after the boulder rolls back down and Sisyphus is able to rest briefly as he walks to the bottom of the hill. If he had no idea that his efforts were pointless, perhaps on the surface it would not seem so tragic. The real punishment is his understanding; yet, at the same time, by understanding his fate he becomes free of it. He ceases to wish for another outcome because he knows it cannot be; he knows his task is pointless and becomes free to create his own meaning. Despair comes from the rejection of one's own reality, longing for a past that no longer exists, or hoping for a future that cannot be. But by acknowledging that the attempt is futile, these "crushing truths" no longer hold the same weight. Camus isn't saying life is devoid of meaning; he is saying the search for meaning outside of our physical existence ultimately leads to disappointment and unhappiness because it will never result in a definitive answer—it is impossible to know if further meaning exists.

> This universe henceforth without a master seems to him neither sterile nor futile. Each atom of that stone, each mineral flake of that night-filled mountain, it itself forms a world. The struggle itself toward the heights is enough to fill a man's heart.

Camus believed we are ultimately responsible for creating meaning in our own lives. "For if there is a sin against life, it consists perhaps not so much in despairing of life as in hoping for another life and in eluding the implacable grandeur of this life." Camus ends his essay with "One must imagine Sisyphus happy." Climate change is the collective boulder we must all push up the hill. And we must be at peace when in rolls back down again. We must find meaning in action itself without the hope of a solution.

Goldilocks Planet

Afterword:
My Summer in Grief

The writing of this collection coincided with our two senior dogs, Bones and Captain (yes, after *Star Trek*) receiving completely different but equally disheartening diagnoses about a week apart. Life became concerned only with vet visits, surgeries, medications, and radiation. Previous to the diagnoses neither had shown signs of slowing down, so the sudden shift in health was a blow. This was followed by more of the same, a deluge of personal tragedies and moments of crisis; everyone and everything seemed to be breaking down all around us, including my own mental health, which reached its lowest point. It felt almost cosmic; I could no longer remember the sensation of receiving good news or any news that wasn't the absolute worst.

At times it was hard to write because I just couldn't care anymore. I was writing about ecological grief, but my own grief was getting in the way. Experiencing a personal crisis made thinking about the broader (but also personal) crisis of climate change feel less immediate. If your own house is on fire, it is doubtful you are thinking about the implications of increased wildfires over time.

One night, in the midst of all this chaos I heard, "I just have to pray." I couldn't tell if the words had awoken me or if I'd happened into consciousness a second before they were uttered. Groggy, I was only somewhat aware that it was Evan, talking in his sleep. I'd never even heard him say the word "pray" before, and the silence that followed only made it stranger.

When I was little, I prayed constantly. They were more like strategically worded wishes, sometimes for material items, sometimes for the punishment of my siblings. As I got a little older, they became superstitious. My dad was always traveling for work, and I believed that if I didn't pray for his safe return, his plane would crash. But one night I fell asleep before I finished praying and he made it home alright, so I stopped.

I detested church. We only attended briefly during my childhood, but the memories feel larger. In Sunday school the teachers would ask what we learned about that week. I was always worried they would call on me and wanted to get ahead of it, so I raised my hand first and blurted out, "Jesus died on the cross for our sins." I said this every single week. I remember their disappointment as they asked if I had more to add and I would respond, "That's it!" I was just relieved I no longer had to speak. It was the only religious-sounding sentence I knew and I had no idea what it meant. It never occurred to me that I should try to come up with something new. A week felt like an eternity to me, and the idea that anyone would remember what I had said the Sunday before seemed impossible. That was pretty much the extent of my religious experience. Aside from a rough patch in high school when I was overcome with guilt for having sex so I attended a random church alone, where I cried and sang with an unreasonable level of enthusiasm, but that was really a one-off.

When things started to fall apart last year, I began praying again. I'm not sure these are prayers either, maybe more of a conversation with the unknown. Sometimes I say thank you, or talk through my worries and ask for guidance. I thought about asking Evan to pray with me, but I figured he didn't need the added anxiety of wondering who he married.

Lying in the dark that night, I wondered if my subconscious had been talking to his, or maybe it was some sort of sign from the universe. I've never been much into signs, except in times of immense grief when they become the only floating object in a sea of anguish. I reached over to hold his hand; though still sleeping soundly, he held mine back and I began to pray. I prayed to the earth, the animals, the universe, God, our ancestors, our descendants, my subconscious, and to extraterrestrials, or whoever might be running the simulation to help us. *Please, please, please, anything, show us anything, a way out of this. How do we cope? How do we survive? We don't have the tools—please share yours!* I prayed myself to sleep that night and many nights after.

On a physical level I can't say much changed, but energetically it's certainly made an impact. I feel less alone. Consciously, I may have assumed I was praying to no one. But even if I was only speaking to my subconscious, at the very least I was acknowledging my grief rather than sweeping it under the rug; someone was out there, even if that someone was me. I realized that as I prayed, I became more grateful—I had so much to pray for. The more I care for the natural world, the less alone I feel. Yes, my life may be falling apart. But so is everything; everyone needs help. Focusing on distant wildfires when your own house is burning may not be an instinctive action, but maybe it's not a bad idea to try (metaphorically, of course).

These are the times when having a strong belief system is the most helpful. The habits of that belief system were formed during better times. Maybe they become like autopilot for a while, and that's okay. Occasionally, it helps to check out mentally, to stop reading about the climate crisis and factory farms, because there's simply too much bad news and emotionally it is sometimes more than the soul can bear. However, even when checking out, the structure of my belief system and my daily actions remain.

I am and always will be a vegan. I look out for the butterflies that get stuck in our screened-in porch and safely escort them back outside. When the extreme cold arrives, I will make sure we have heat lamps, pads, and shelter for the opossums, raccoons, and feral cats. In the summer I'll make sure there is shade and fresh water for any visitors. When an animal is struck and killed by a passing car, I will bury them in my garden as if they were my own. And I will continue to do so until it all matters again.

Chop Wood, Carry Water

Acknowledgments

I am profoundly grateful to my partner, Evan Kaspar, and to the animals with whom we share our home. Evan has contributed so much to these essays by simply being himself. His compassion for all living beings is remarkable, and I learn from him every day. I don't know what I would do without his singing, which makes our home cheerful even on the dreariest of days. Captain, Bones, Tati, Monte, and Chilly have each impacted my life beyond words. I am so lucky to be the caretaker of such magnificent beings who have taught me true unconditional love, make me laugh, and break my heart all at once.

I would be lost without the smell of the ocean, the quaking aspens in autumn, the dappled shade of a redwood, and the smell of Texas sage. I am forever indebted to the orb weavers for making their return each June; the hummingbirds who visit the flame acanthus outside my window and who have become gentle reminders of loved ones lost; the heavy snowfall that softens all sounds; and the neighborhood cats who play on the front porch.

I am so fortunate to have Jay Bugg and Cathy Bugg as parents, who have always encouraged me to follow my own path, however winding it may seem. Thank you to Dorothy Jones and my grandparents, who each have a place in my heart whenever I smell pine trees, pick tomatoes off the vine, dive into a cold lake, or a ladybug lands on my shoulder.

Thank you to Tom Doran, whose guidance served as a constant reminder to be authentic and to always keep learning and trying. There have been many wonderful teachers, writers, visual artists, and friends in my life who have offered their wisdom, encouragement, and critique. Many thanks to Drew Smith, James Lough, Chloé Allyn, Lauren Richter, Lucy Spelman, Elizabeth Maynard, Jason Grear, George Gross, Patrick Weaver, Romia Ernst, J. Chris Wong, Mack Patterson, Talia Garrido, Carmen Moreno, Margaret Broughton, Casey Merkle, Namita Dharia, Sean Nesselrode Moncada, Mairéad Byrne, Jonathan Highfield, Jenny Kuhla, Stephen Geller, Joel Fleschman, Jeff Kessel, Josh Justice, Kate Faulk, Stacy Dunavan, Amanda Depperschmidt, Cy White, Mike Ryan, Brian Normoyle and everyone at Lantern Publishing & Media, as well as so many others who have added to my life and education with warmth and understanding. Special thanks to my editor, Gregory Brown, for his ability to work through this collection with patience, skill, and enthusiasm.

Notes

1 Cunsolo, Ashlee, and Neville R. Ellis. "Ecological Grief as a Mental Health Response to Climate Change-Related Loss," *Nature Climate Change* 8 (2018), 275–281.

2 Leopold, Aldo. *A Sand County Almanac: And Sketches Here and There*, with an introduction by Barbara Kingsolver (New York: Oxford University Press, 2020).

3 United States Environmental Protection Agency. "Evaluating Developmental Neurotoxicity Hazard: Better than Before," *Science Matters* (last updated November 21, 2023), https://www.epa.gov/sciencematters/evaluating-developmental-neurotoxicity-hazard-better.

4 Murphy, Michelle. "Alterlife and Decolonial Chemical Relations," *Cultural Anthropology* 32, no. 4 (2017): 494–503.

5 Klein, Ezra. "You Kids Are Not Doomed," *New York Times*, June 5, 2022. https://www.nytimes.com/2022/06/05/opinion/climate-change-should-you-have-kids.html.

6 Quammen, David. *Spillover: Animal Infections and the Next Human Pandemic* (New York: W. W. Norton, 2012).

7 Ryden, Hope. *Lily Pond: Four Years with a Family of Beavers* (New York: Lyons & Burford, 1989).

8 Tova, Elisabeth. *The Sound of a Wild Snail Eating* (Chapel Hill, NC: Algonquin Books of Chapel Hill, 2016).

9   Chang, Kenneth. "In Hawaii, Chickens Gone Wild," *New York Times*, April 6, 2015. https://www.nytimes.com/2015/04/07/science/in-hawaii-chickens-gone-wild.html.

10   Kimmerer, Robin Wall. *Braiding Sweetgrass* (Minneapolis: Milkweed Editions, 2013).

11   Sagan, Carl. *The Cosmic Connection* (London, UK: Hodder & Stoughton, 1973).

12   Ehrlich, Paul, and Brian Walker. "Rivets and Redundancy," *BioScience* 48, no. 5 (1998): 387. https://link.gale.com/apps/doc/A20924871/HRCA?u=anon~6d0ca44a&sid=googleScholar&xid=68eb10be.

13   Ahmad, Rubaiya. "Why Animal-Rights Is Not a Luxury: Rubaiya Ahmad at TEDxDhaka," September 21, 2013, YouTube video, 21:51,https://www.youtube.com/watch?v=ixGoULHxD98&t=21s.

14   Kimmerer. *Braiding Sweetgrass*, 167–174.

15   Garber, Megan. "The Dark Side of the Houseplant Boom," *The Atlantic*, April 20, 2021. https://www.theatlantic.com/culture/archive/2021/04/dark-side-houseplant-boom-nature-empathy/618638/.

16   Kondo, Marie. *The Life-Changing Magic of Tidying Up: The Japanese Art of Decluttering and Organizing* (Berkeley, CA: Ten Speed Press, 2014).

17   Livingston, Julie. *Self-Devouring Growth: A Planetary Parable* (Durham, NC: Duke University Press, 2019).

18   *My Octopus Teacher*, directed by Pippa Ehrlich and James Reed (Los Gatos, CA: Netflix, 2020).

19   Muir, John. "The Yosemite National Park," *The Atlantic*, August 1899. https://www.theatlantic.com/magazine/archive/1899/08/the-yosemite-national-park/307403/.

20   Owen, Russell. "John Muir and the Edenic Narrative: Towards an Understanding of Class and Racial Bias in the Writing of a Preeminent Environmentalist" (graduate thesis, University of Montana, 1998), https://scholarworks.umt.edu/cgi/viewcontent.cgi?article=7660&context=etd.

21 *Planet Earth*, directed by Alastair Fothergill and Mark Linfield (New York: BBC Worldwide Americas, 2006).

22 Marris, Emma. "Nature Is Everywhere—We Just Need to Learn to See It | Emma Marris," TED, August 19, 2016, YouTube video, 15:52, https://www.youtube.com/watch?v=hiIcwt88o94.

23 Marris, Emma. *Rambunctious Garden* (New York: Bloomsbury, 2013).

24 Cohen, Thierry. "Darkened Cities," photography collection (Monségur, France, 2019), https://thierrycohen.com/pages/work/starlights.html.

25 Kesebir, Selin, and Pelin Kesebir. "A Growing Disconnection from Nature Is Evident in Cultural Products," *Perspectives on Psychological Science* 12, no. 2 (2017): 258–269. https://doi.org/10.1177/1745691616662473.

26 "Definition of Veganism," The Vegan Society, 1988. https://www.vegansociety.com/go-vegan/definition-veganism.

27 Blanchette, Alex. *Porkopolis: American Animality, Standardized Life, and the Factory Farm* (Durham, NC: Duke University Press, 2020).

28 Singer, Peter. "Peter Singer: The Why and How of Effective Altruism," TED, May 20, 2013, YouTube video, 17:20, https://www.youtube.com/watch?v=Diuv3XZQXyc.

29 Camus, Albert. *The Myth of Sisyphus & Other Essays* (New York: Random House, 1955).

About the Author

 **Jess Bugg** is a writer and artist based in Austin, TX. She blends her passion for ecology and animal rights with a love of storytelling. Bugg received her BA in visual communication from the Savannah College of Art and Design with concentrations in photography and writing. She received her MA in nature-culture-sustainability studies from the Rhode Island School of Design. She is trained in classical Pilates and teaches with a focus on chronic illness and rehabilitation.

About the Publisher

Lantern Publishing & Media was founded in 2020 to follow and expand on the legacy of Lantern Books—a publishing company started in 1999 on the principles of living with a greater depth and commitment to the preservation of the natural world. Like its predecessor, Lantern Publishing & Media produces books on animal advocacy, veganism, religion, social justice, humane education, psychology, family therapy, and recovery. Lantern is dedicated to printing in the United States on recycled paper and saving resources in our day-to-day operations. Our titles are also available as ebooks and audiobooks.

To catch up on Lantern's publishing program, visit us at www.lanternpm.org.

facebook.com/lanternpm
instagram.com/lanternpm
tiktok.com/@lanternpmofficial